Student Success

How to Make It Happen

Frederic Skoglund and Judy Ness

ROWMAN & LITTLEFIELD EDUCATION
A division of
ROWMAN & LITTLEFIELD PUBLISHERS, INC.
Lanham • New York • Toronto • Plymouth, UK

Published by Rowman & Littlefield Education
A division of Rowman & Littlefield Publishers, Inc.
A wholly owned subsidiary of The Rowman & Littlefield Publishing Group, Inc.
4501 Forbes Boulevard, Suite 200, Lanham, Maryland 20706
http://www.rowmaneducation.com

Estover Road, Plymouth PL6 7PY, United Kingdom

British Library Cataloguing in Publication Information Available

Library of Congress Cataloging-in-Publication Data

Skoglund, Frederic, 1945–
  Student success : how to make it happen / Frederic Skoglund, Judy Ness.
    p. cm.
  Includes bibliographical references.
  ISBN 978-1-61048-354-4 (cloth : alk. paper) — ISBN 978-1-61048-355-1 (pbk. : alk. paper) — ISBN 978-1-61048-356-8 (electronic)
  1. School improvement programs—United States. 2. Academic achievement—United States. 3. Public schools—United States. I. Ness, Judy, 1942– II. Title.
  LB2822.82.S48 2011
  371.200973—dc22   2011002319

♾™ The paper used in this publication meets the minimum requirements of American National Standard for Information Sciences—Permanence of Paper for Printed Library Materials, ANSI/NISO Z39.48-1992.

Printed in the United States of America

Contents

Foreword

Lawrence W. Lezotte, PhD

Executive Vice President, Effective Schools Products Ltd.

We have all heard of or played the parlor game where one person whispers something to the person sitting next to him and the secret is passed along until all have been told. Generally, when the final person tells what was last heard, the original message has been substantially distorted. School improvement is no "parlor game" to be sure but effective practices often travel from school to school and teacher to teacher with similar message distortion and disintegration as it is passed down the line from one educator to the next. The message disintegration problem is especially critical when the "proven practices" of one school or teacher are passed along through what would be described as "over-the-back-fence conversations."

The Effective Schools research movement has been accurately described as a "practitioners' movement" because it began about 40 years ago with rich descriptions of school and classroom practices that worked to advance the learning of all students in those settings. The Effective Schools research has continued to evolve and incorporate a diverse array of school types. We now know more about what and how to make other schools effective because of the steady accumulation of descriptions of effective practices. Like most educators familiar with this body of work, I marvel at the consistency of the factors that have been repeatedly found to be associated with improving student achievement.

The Effective Schools and effective teaching research continues to enjoy wide popularity with practicing educators because it makes sense. These two interrelated bodies of research have captured the "wisdom" of successful practitioners from many different settings and made it available to others.

I was pleased to accept the invitation to write the foreword to *Student Success: How to Make It Happen* because it represents a valuable addition to this large and growing body of work. The book not only precisely communicates what more effective schools have done, but it also details precisely how they did it, and provides the means for others to do it. The authors, Frederic Skoglund and Judy Ness, have demonstrated that effective strategies in one setting do work effectively in others, if and when they are implemented with fidelity, using the proven tools offered in the book.

The authors are both career educators who have been successful in a variety of different roles. As proven practitioners they are able to bring the problems that routinely confront schools and classrooms into sharp focus. In addition, they have proven themselves to be serious students of the effective school and teacher research. Most importantly, they have integrated the research and proven practices into a cohesive set of action steps that have been successfully implemented in many schools.

It is one thing for school leaders and leadership teams to be committed to improving student achievement; it's another to know what to do to make it happen in their schools. *Student Success: How to Make It Happen* provides an answer for these educators. This book presents the research on which the practices are based. It provides clear and precise details for how any school should proceed. Finally, and perhaps most significantly, it includes the actual process tools needed to ensure that the mission of "learning for all" shifts from a dream to a reality.

Authors Skoglund and Ness have made sure that their message will not disintegrate or be distorted if schools follow their framework, processes, and tools. If educators who say they are committed to the mission of "learning for all" are still unable to take appropriate action after reading this book, they should take a second look at the depth of their commitment.

Chapter One

Getting Started

WHY, WHO, AND HOW WELL

Why the Continuous Improvement System?

In answer to this opening question we borrow these words from *The Tale of Two Cities*, "It was the best of times, it was the worst of times," and we apply them to the current conditions in education. It is the best of times because we have an amazing collection of tried-and-true research resulting in practices and models we know work. In addition, we have some innovative and new research and models that are helping us change and improve our practice. It is the worst of times because confidence in our public schools is at an all-time low and funding is decreasing at an alarming rate.

We wrote this book because we want to share the power of the Continuous Improvement System (CIS).[1] We have created the System by combining some of the best findings from the tried-and-true research with the most powerful findings of the innovative and new. The CIS differs from segmented approaches to school improvement in that it functions with a holistic view of the school. In this book we share a step-by-step process for implementing and sustaining the System.

The CIS significantly benefits the school because it:

1. Builds and sustains a culture of excellence that is focused on teaching and learning.
2. Views the school as a complex whole that is comprised of multiple integrated components.

---

1. Throughout the book the Continuous Improvement System will appear as its full title, CIS, or the System.

1

3. Helps administrators and teachers improve their professional practice.
4. Helps faculty members change the culture of their school from individual professionals working in isolation to a collaborative culture focused on improving student learning.
5. Improves student performance as measured by student scores on high-stakes tests.

The Continuous Improvement System is not the long-sought-after "silver bullet." We do not think there is such a bullet. What we do know from our experience is that when the leaders and teachers in a school apply the System described in this book with fidelity, both student achievement and teacher performance improve. We have both quantitative and qualitative data to support that statement.

Who Needs the Continuous Improvement System?

We answer this question with a somewhat bold statement:

> Every educator who wants to improve student achievement should implement the Continuous Improvement System.

We wrote this book with three specific groups in mind. These are:

- School- and district-level administrators
- Teachers at all grade levels and in all content areas
- Students

We know that the System described in this book requires an active partnership among these three groups. Administrators and teachers work together to implement and apply the System with their goal being the improvement of their individual and collective practice. As they do this, they are not doing things *to* the students. They are doing things *with* the students. All three groups partner with each other, and the shared purpose for these groups is improved student learning.

How Do We Know It Works?

The Continuous Improvement System is comprised of components developed by researchers over a period of many years. Although we have introduced individual components at both the elementary and secondary levels, our most recent work has been devoted to combining these components into the complete

System that is the subject of this book. Beginning in the 2005–2006 school year, we have worked with 17 elementary schools located in the Phoenix, Arizona, metropolitan area to implement the complete System. We see this work as only a beginning.

We realize that this is a very small sample and additional data must be collected to statistically prove the effectiveness of the System over time. The effectiveness of the System, however, should not be discounted simply because the work is new and the sample is small. The gains in student achievement in the sample schools are so clear and the experiences described by administrators and teachers are so positive, that we firmly believe the System will make a difference in any school in any state and even in international schools when implemented with fidelity. We know the System described in this book works. We have seen it work. We have real-life stories that demonstrate that it works.

The Arizona Department of Education conducts an end-of-year high-stakes test called the Arizona Instrument to Measure Standards (AIMS). All data shown in table 1.1 are from the Arizona Department of Education AIMS records and indicate the percentage of students who achieved scores in either the "Meets State Standards" or "Exceeds State Standards" categories. Due to the fact that six of the schools began their projects in 2009 and because the Arizona Department of Education changed the AIMS test to reflect new state standards three times from 2002 to 2010, only 11 of our 17 sample schools have valid comparable data. All 11 schools showed improved student achievement in reading and in math.

Table 1.1 Impact of the Continuous Improvement System

SCHOOL	PROJECT BEGAN	PRIOR YEAR AIMS		PROJECT ENDED	END YEAR AIMS	
		Math	Reading		Math	Reading
B. A. B. School	February 2007	62	49	May 2008	77	61
C. W. School	June 2007	43	41	April 2010**	73	72
A. F. G. School	August 2005*	53	45	May 2009	54	49
A. M. H. School	December 2006	27	31	May 2009	65	65
J. L. K. School	October 2005*	48	42	May 2009	59	62
M. School	June 2007	57	54	April 2010**	66	66
O. School	August 2006	51	52	May 2009	67	59
O. W. School	November 2008	51	52	Ongoing**	60	63
S. B. School	October 2008	42	46	Ongoing**	60	52
W. R. S. School	October 2006	41	34	May 2009	57	50
W. School	August 2006	40	40	May 2009	67	58

* The Arizona Department of Education changed math and reading tests between the 2004 and the 2005 school year; therefore the score reported is from the end of the first year of the project.
** The Arizona Department of Education changed the math test between the 2009 and the 2010 school year; therefore the score reported is from the final year of the 2005–2009 test.

Accepting the fact that at this point in time there is little statistical data available, we suggest that you read the book and then ask yourself, "Does this make sense to me?" If it does, we hope that you will try the System for a couple of reasons. First, we believe that you will like the result. Second, we want you to get in touch with us to share your stories and your data so that the statistical analysis can continue.

BEFORE WE BEGIN

We want to note four things:

- We are very aware of and concerned about gender bias. On the other hand, we are also aware that the use of he/she and him/her significantly interrupts the flow of printed or spoken messages. Consequently, we have chosen to use the pronoun "he" to represent both genders.
- Throughout the book, we have primarily used an example of elementary mathematics to explain the Continuous Improvement System. We have done this because we believe that the use of one consistent example makes it easier for readers to learn and understand the CIS.
- We suggest that initially you scan the book in its entirety to gain a big-picture perspective. Then carefully read it a second time, to gain a comprehensive understanding of the details of the System. After reading each chapter, take the time to reflect on what you have read and consider which of the Effective Schools Correlates and/or Systems Disciplines are at work in the chapter.
- Templates for all charts and forms are available at Viking Solutions (vikingsolutions.net).

Chapter Two

An Overview of the
Continuous Improvement System

THE FOUNDATION

Throughout the book, we have included stories to demonstrate the impact of the Continuous Improvement System on administrators, teachers, and students. Here is one of those stories.

A SUCCESS STORY

One of the first schools in the Phoenix area to implement the Continuous Improvement System is located in a high-poverty area. The school serves a student population that is 98 percent minority and 96 percent of the students receive services under the free/ reduced lunch program.

When Fred began to work with the school, the school had failed to meet the Annual Yearly Progress (AYP) requirement under the federal No Child Left Behind law for three years. The school was also identified as Underperforming in the Arizona Learns rating system during this same time.

At the beginning of the 2008-2009 school year, the principal and the faculty made a commitment to fully implement the Continuous Improvement System. They lived up to their commitment and, after the state tests were administered in May of 2009, the school was rated as Performing Plus under AZ Learns and missed making AYP due to a single reading score in one grade level.

The following is an excerpt from a letter to the principal from a representative of the School Improvement and Intervention Unit of the Arizona Department of Education.

"I just wanted to share with you how enjoyable and refreshing it was to visit your campus yesterday. I visit schools all over the state and it is rare to see so much improvement in so many areas in a relatively short amount of time. It is evident that a culture of organization, respect, professionalism, communication, collaboration and data driven instruction is developing."

The principal is now a firm supporter of the CIS and states, "I have learned from some great people – Lezotte, Hunter, Marzano, Covey and Chaplin to name a few – but I was not able to connect all of this information until Dr. Skoglund brought the Continuous Improvement System to our school. This has changed our school culture and improved the level of our students' academic achievement."

THE CONTINUOUS IMPROVEMENT SYSTEM: BASED ON SOLID RESEARCH

The CIS is based on two powerful compilations of research. The first is the Correlates of the Effective Schools identified by Edmonds, Brookover, and Lezotte (1978). The second is the Five Disciplines of Learning Organizations identified by Senge (1990). Because we consider a basic understanding of this research essential to the successful implementation of the System, a summary of their findings follows.

The Effective Schools Movement

In the early 1960s, the U.S. Office of Education funded research by James Coleman. His 1966 paper, *Equality of Educational Opportunity*, became known as the Coleman Report in which he concluded that public schools did not make a significant difference in the education of their students. He stated that a student's success in school was predetermined by the student's family background. Based on his findings he stated that poor families lacked the prime conditions and values that support academic success and as a result students from poor families could not learn, regardless of what the school did.

Dr. Edmonds of Harvard University and Drs. Brookover and Lezotte of Michigan State University immediately acknowledged that family background did have an impact, but they refused to accept that schools did not make a difference. They identified schools in several cities where students from poverty were academically successful. As a result of this investigation, they identified several characteristics that were common to schools where students were achieving academically. Because these characteristics were directly correlated with student success, they became known as the Effective Schools Correlates and led to the foundational belief of the Effective Schools movement—learning for all.

These correlates cover every aspect of a school. There is nothing that happens in the daily operation of a school that cannot be addressed under one of the correlates. However, it is important to note that no correlate stands alone. Instead, they are an integrated set of research findings that lead educators to view the school as of a complex whole—a system of interdependent components. We use this system of correlates as a foundation of the CIS.

Each correlate has a first and second generation. The first generation is a result of the original research done by Edmonds, Brookover, and Lezotte. The second generation was created to help schools that had successfully implemented the first generation and were ready to take the next step in the school improvement process. Because they are sequential, the second generation cannot be implemented until the first generation is in place. The correlates are:

Clear and Focused Mission **First generation:** There is a clearly articulated school mission that the staff understands and is committed to accomplish. The mission expresses that the faculty accepts the responsibility for all students' learning.

Second generation: There is a distinct shift toward an appropriate balance between basic skills and higher-level learning.

Instructional Leadership **First generation:** The principal acts as an instructional leader and effectively communicates the mission to all who are involved in the educational process. The principal ensures instructional effectiveness.

Second generation: The act of leadership is broadened to include the teaching faculty and focuses on creating a community of shared values.

Opportunity to Learn and Student Time on Task **First generation:** A significant amount of classroom time is devoted to teacher-directed learning activities focused on essential skills.

Second generation: A process of organized abandonment occurs in order to address the problem of too much to teach and not enough time to do so. Nothing new can be added until current practices are evaluated and unnecessary and ineffective practices are discarded. Collaboration and interdisciplinary curricula become critical.

Frequent Monitoring of Student Progress **First generation:** Student progress is frequently monitored and the data are used to improve individual student performance and the instructional program.

Second generation: More attention is paid to the alignment between the written, the taught, and the tested curricula. The monitoring of student progress emphasizes more authentic assessments. Students play an important role in monitoring their own progress.

High Expectations for Success   **First generation:** The faculty believes they have the capability to help all students attain mastery of the essential skills, and they do their work in a manner that demonstrates that belief.

Second generation: Schools are transformed from being a place of teaching to a place where learning is assured. There are high performance expectations for the faculty as well as for the students, and there is a willingness among these members of the learning community to work to meet these expectations.

Safe, Orderly, and Caring Environment   **First generation:** There is an orderly, purposeful, and businesslike environment that is free from the threat of physical harm and conducive to teaching and learning.

Second generation: The focus shifts from the absence of undesirable student behavior to the presence of desirable behaviors. A healthy respect for human diversity, psychological safety, and the importance of collaboration is evident.

Home–School Relations   **First generation:** Parents understand and support the school's basic mission.

Second generation: Parent involvement moves past lip service and communication flows freely in both directions, resulting in an authentic partnership between the school and the home.

Research on the correlates has continued over the years and has received renewed attention in recent years due to the national concern about student achievement. Taylor, Pressley, and Pearson (2002) summarized findings from five extensive studies on high-poverty but effective elementary schools. They reported:

- Improved student learning was an overriding priority.
- Principals, teachers, and parents cited a collective sense of responsibility.
- Strong building leadership was critical to school improvement.
- Teachers planned and taught together with a focus on how to best meet student needs.
- Ongoing professional development focused on research-supported practice was evident.
- Teachers in successful schools consistently study student assessment data and use the data as a basis to work together to refine instruction.

These findings are consistent with past Effective Schools research and demonstrate the staying power of the correlates.

The Systems Disciplines

In addition to the Effective Schools Correlates, successful implementation of the CIS requires the effective use of the five disciplines identified by noted systems scholar Dr. Peter Senge. His research clearly demonstrates that the use of these disciplines is critical to the successful functioning of any organization. The use of these disciplines helps educators to become more skilled in thinking and functioning systemically. The five disciplines are:

Shared Vision

The vision is the image of the organization that people aspire to achieve. It is a clear picture that gives people direction for their work. It occurs when the people of an organization choose to pursue a common goal. It may evolve from a single person's idea but it cannot be imposed on others. It must be willingly embraced by the vast majority of the people within the organization if the vision is to become their reality.

There is a powerful example in our fairly recent history that demonstrates the power of a shared vision. Think back to John F. Kennedy's inaugural speech. What most people remember is the quote "Ask not what your country can do for you; ask what you can do for your country." This was a great sound bite for the media but it did little to change the country. However, in the same speech he made a statement that changed not only the country but the world. He said that we would put a man on the moon before the end of the decade. This single statement drove the work of every person at NASA for the next several years. People pursued this vision with passion, not because they had to, but because they chose to embrace the shared vision.

In a school a shared vision serves as a filter for decisions. It is set out in the school vision statement and ensures that improvement planning is truly focused on helping all students succeed. It sets parameters and becomes a consistent beacon to help faculty members refocus when the inevitable disruptions occur.

Personal Mastery

Personal mastery is exactly what the name implies. It is the pursuit of a personal dream. It requires a commitment to the learning, personal growth, and hard work required to successfully realize that dream.

This concept is reflected in the U.S. Army slogan—Be All That You Can Be. Personal mastery is what happens when an individual chooses to do all that is necessary to achieve a personal dream. It is seen in the behavior of athletes like Michael Jordan, scholars like Stephen Hawking, and business entrepreneurs like Bill Gates.

When a teacher pursues advanced degrees, takes part in professional development activities, reads professional journals, and frequently engages colleagues in dialogue with the sole intent of becoming a more effective teacher, the teacher is demonstrating the desire to achieve personal mastery. No one can force another to pursue personal mastery, but the effective principal will create the conditions under which teachers will choose to seek personal mastery.

Mental Models

Mental models are the lenses through which we each view the world. They are the beliefs that result from the accumulation of our learning and our life experiences. They strongly influence our thinking and the decisions we make.

Recognizing mental models is important because they drive our behaviors. For example, divergent mental models cause Congress to become bogged down in partisan political behavior and drive religious fanatics to acts of terrorism. When we recognize and understand our mental models, we can prevent their presence from having an unconscious and negative impact on our decisions and behaviors. On the positive side, when organizational members understand their mental models, they have a better opportunity to target their energy and efforts on the shared vision. It is particularly important for leaders to recognize and address the mental models of those they lead as they seek to develop a diverse group of individuals into an effective and cohesive team.

Sadly, some educators still accept Coleman's conclusion that some students either cannot or will not learn. This is a destructive mental model that will prevent the teacher from being effective in the classroom. When a principal recognizes this mental model at work, the principal must follow one of two paths with the teacher. The principal can involve the teacher in carefully planned experiences that will allow the teacher to choose to adopt a more positive mental model. If this is not successful, the principal must remove the teacher from the classroom.

Team Learning

This is the phenomenon that occurs when individuals engage in a dialogue that raises the collective knowledge of the group beyond that of any individual member of the group. It results in the whole becoming greater than the sum of the parts. It is an effective antidote to the isolation experienced by educators in schools across the United States.

Team learning occurs when a group of Microsoft programmers come together to design a new product. Each individual within the group brings his own ideas to the dialogue. The ideas are shared, discussed, accepted, rejected, and improved in the creation of the final product. Team learning also occurs when a group of teachers looks at data and then generates strategies to address the issue identified by the data.

Currently in education, we are investing a considerable amount of resources in the development and support of learning communities. The CIS requires four different types of learning communities: the implementation team, the leadership team, the instructional team, and the faculty as a whole. When these teams function effectively, they become the heart and soul of the CIS.

Systems Thinking

This is the ability to see the interconnectedness of the individual components of an organization as an integrated whole. It clarifies the relationships among the individual components.

Systems thinking is a supervisor's ability to understand that the installation of a new computer system has implications for software compatibility, personnel training, and support services. It is a principal's ability to make the connections between the curriculum, the instruction, the assessments, and the data analysis that is used to drive instruction. When people engage in systems thinking, they realize that no component of an organization stands alone. As a result, people are able to plan and implement change in one component of a system with the implications of this change on the other components clearly in mind.

Systems thinking is central to the success of the Continuous Improvement System. One cannot implement CIS without it. Systems thinking allows a principal to anticipate how the implementation of a new curriculum will require changes in the formative assessment process. Thinking through a systems lens will also help the principal involve faculty members in professional development activities that meet their immediate needs as they work together to implement the new curriculum. This kind of thinking highlights the need for collaboration and emphasizes that every part of a system impacts every other part of the system. It clearly demonstrates the fact that nothing stands alone.

THE CONTINUOUS IMPROVEMENT SYSTEM MODEL

Earlier in this chapter we stated that the Correlates of Effective Schools based on the research by Brookover, Edmonds, and Lezotte, as well as Senge's work on systems and learning organizations, form the cornerstone for the

Continuous Improvement System. As you study the conceptual model shown in figure 2.1, take time to reflect on what you have just read and identify the correlate(s) and/or the discipline(s) that are at work in each component of the model.

The desired level of student achievement is expressed as the:

| Academic mission |

The academic mission is pursued by teachers who work in:

| Instructional Teams |

The instructional teams are guided by:

| Core Commitments |

The instructional teams accomplish their work through a structured:

| Operational Sequence |

The operational sequence includes components of:

| Leadership | Curriculum & Instruction | Formative Assessment | Achievement Data | Accountability |

Under these components, educators use:

| • Scheduled Meetings | • Instructional Calendars
 • Instructional Strategies & Materials | • Common Assessments
 • Error Analysis | • Individual & Collective Achievement Data | • Personnel Evaluation
 • Professional Development |

Figure 2.1   The Components of the Continuous Improvement System

Chapter Three

Implementation

THE GAME PLAN

How Do You Implement the CIS in the School?

Successful implementation of the Continuous Improvement System (CIS) is not easy and it is not quick. It requires attention to detail and a relentless demand to do things right—*every time*. This demand must be accompanied by the training and support necessary to assist people in meeting the demand. The following sequence of six steps provides the school with an effective and efficient process for successfully implementing the Continuous Improvement System.

Step 1: Involve District-level Administrators

Before beginning the work at the school level the principal must clearly communicate the desire to implement the CIS to the appropriate district-level administrators and get their approval for the work. The direct supervisor of the principal must be a part of this conversation. This first step is very important because the district-level administrators play a critical role in providing the needed resources for implementation and in giving the principal the flexibility to implement a new system that may not follow all of the current district procedures.

Step 2: Involve Key Staff Members Early On

Once district-level approval has been granted, the principal meets with the most trusted and respected members of the faculty and provides them with a clear overview of the CIS. He also shows examples of results achieved in other schools where the System has been implemented. This group serves as an implementation team. When the principal is sure he has the complete support of all the members of the implementation team, they work together to plan and present a clear and comprehensive orientation of the CIS to the entire faculty. In some cases this presentation may require more than the time available in the typical faculty meeting schedule. There needs to be enough time to ensure that all staff members have a clear understanding of the purpose and the process of the CIS at the end of this meeting. During the presentation meeting, members of the implementation team sit with each of the small groups and facilitate a conversation to address concerns, answer questions, and gather suggestions from the faculty members. To effectively facilitate these small groups, implementation team members should fully understand the skills of dialogue and advocacy. Both skills are described in chapter 4.

Step 3: Lay the Groundwork for Action

In this step, the faculty creates key documents that provide the foundation for the remaining steps. We suggest creating them in the following order:

- Academic Mission—a description of the target that the educators want to accomplish
- Core Commitments—the actions everyone agrees to take in order to accomplish the academic mission
- Meeting Norms—a description of how the educators will treat each other as they work within the system
- School Rules—a minimal number of expected behaviors exhibited by all students and faculty members
- School Vision—A clear picture of the desired future of the school

Each of these documents is discussed in chapter 6 along with a process for creating them.

Step 4: Create Instructional Calendars and Common Assessments

The instructional calendar is a curriculum planning tool that assists teachers in scheduling their instruction to ensure a consistent focus and timeline. This consistency makes it possible for teachers to create common assessments that are directly linked to curriculum standards and used by all teachers of the same content to frequently measure student achievement. These tools are created during the month following the completion of the academic mission and core commitments noted in step 3. As a result, during the initial part of the implementation process, faculty members will be working on some parts of step 3 and step 4 at the same time.

Step 5: Create and Begin Using Data Charts

In this step, teachers create and implement the following charts:

- Classroom Performance Charts—a measure of the performance of the entire class
- Student Performance Charts—a measure of the performance of an individual student
- Grade-level or Content-area Performance Charts—a measure of the performance of grade-level students or students from different classes studying the same content.

These charts are explained in chapter 10.

Step 6: Meet Regularly and Use an Agenda

The instructional teams, the leadership team, and the full faculty meet regularly. Their focus in every meeting is improved teacher performance and enhanced student learning. The dialogue that occurs in these meetings is a significant factor that helps change the culture of the school from one of isolation and individual practice to a culture of collaboration. Chapter 4 describes skills that help ensure effective use of time and talent during a meeting. Chapter 5 provides examples of meeting agendas that help ensure the focus stays on improved teacher performance and enhanced student learning.

How Do You Implement the CIS District-wide?

We fully recognize that change occurs in one school at a time. However, we also feel a strong sense of urgency to spread the CIS across as many schools as possible so that all teachers and students may experience the success that comes from its implementation. Therefore, once the Continuous Improvement System is functioning successfully within a given school, the district should explore the possibility of taking it district-wide, using the successful school as a demonstration site. This allows the faculty from other schools to see the CIS working with real students and real teachers in real time.

If the concept of "all schools in the district" is too large an undertaking, the district might consider starting with constituent schools of the same instructional level as the school that has successfully implemented the CIS. If that was an elementary school, the next step would be to implement the System in several, if not all, of the elementary schools.

Even after demonstrating successful improvements in student learning and effective change of teaching practices, it may be difficult to transfer the change practices from one instructional level to another. Typical responses from teachers or principals are "That will never work at my level" and "That will never work in my content area." Here are some suggestions for overcoming this possible resistance:

- Begin from the premise that good organization is applicable at any level. The same is true for good teaching.
- Schedule meetings in non–Continuous Improvement System schools of the same instructional level. During these meetings, have the principal, some teachers, and some students from the CIS school talk about how the CIS has impacted them. Hearing students talk about how they are learning more effectively can be a very strong motivator for change.
- Schedule visits to a CIS school for staff from non–CIS schools. Make the visit long enough to ensure that visiting faculty can see teachers using the System in their classrooms and attend a meeting where teachers discuss the grade-level or content-area data charts. Encourage visiting staff to talk to students and ask about their student performance charts.
- Create a partnership between the initial CIS school and a school from the next instructional level up or down. For example, an elementary school and a middle school could partner, or a middle school and a high school could partner. In this scenario, the principals and some teachers from these two schools meet to discuss how to "move" the CIS from the initial school to the partner school.
- Have the principals of the CIS schools conduct a panel or fishbowl discussion about their experience with the System during district leadership team meetings. They could talk about their personal process in implementing the System.
- Have a team of students from a CIS school attend a district leadership team meeting and share how the CIS has helped them improve as learners.
- Interview the principals, teachers, and students from the CIS schools for ideas about how to initiate the System in other schools in the district.
- Invite faculty and students from the initial CIS school to create a video advocating the use of the System in other district schools.

The Effective Schools research has clearly demonstrated that schools control the critical variables necessary to ensure that all students can and will learn, given an appropriate opportunity. The Continuous Improvement

System provides the blueprint for building that opportunity for every student. However, generating such a fundamental change in the culture of a school and a district takes time and effort. It requires a real commitment from all the people who will experience the change. The optimal way of gaining this commitment is to fully involve the people in the planning and implementation of a new approach to the work of ensuring learning for all students. This personal involvement is essential as it is the source of the necessary buy-in that sustains the change over time.

In the following chapter we describe how to create this personal involvement and gain the commitment of everyone involved in the learning mission.

Chapter Four

Leadership

PROVIDING THE SUPPORT STRUCTURE:
WHO DOES IT AND HOW

Who Provides the Support?

There are two primary leaders whose support is essential to the successful implementation of the Continuous Improvement System. These two are the building principal and the superintendent. In this chapter we provide a general description of their unique support responsibilities and the specific supports each must provide.

The Principal

The Effective Schools research clearly defines the role of the principal as the instructional leader of the school. This role requires that he devote substantial time and effort to monitor and improve the quality of instruction in every classroom. He must demand effective instruction and continuously demonstrate the value of data as a clear indicator of the level of student learning. In addition, he must ensure that teachers receive the support they need to meet his high expectations. Because of the enormity of this task, the principal cannot do it alone.

Therefore, he must become the facilitator of a system that generates a sense of purpose and responsibility that is shared by everyone within the school. This requires clarity and commitment. Everyone in the school must clearly understand that the learning-for-all mission from the Effective Schools literature means teachers will continuously work to ensure the success of every student. That is the clarity. The commitment is everyone agrees that the success of every student is nonnegotiable. Every teacher in partnership with the principal and the students works to make that student success a reality. No one can choose not to work toward the realization of the mission.

The Superintendent

When a school district leader assists the schools in learning and applying the CIS, the economy of scale is significant. There are many ways a superintendent can support the use of the System in the schools across the district. He can direct district office personnel to organize their work around providing this support. Learning for all children should be the focus at both the school level and the district level. This includes departments like Human Resources, Finance, and Transportation. All school and district personnel must agree to hold themselves and each other accountable for meeting this expectation.

He can visit schools, encouraging teachers and principals as they learn about and then apply the CIS. He can organize his leadership team to support the CIS. He can help schools celebrate their successes. He can communicate about the CIS to the school board.

While this book is primarily a handbook for the principal and teacher leaders to use as they implement the CIS, it can also provide superintendents with powerful ideas about how to support the use of the System in their districts.

OUR VIEW OF LEADERSHIP

If you ask a room full of people to write their individual definitions of leadership, the responses will vary widely. These varied definitions can cause problems because the different definitions represent different expectations and different expectations result in different actions. Therefore, we suggest that a shared definition of leadership is essential when trying to improve teaching and learning in a school. In the Continuous Improvement System we use the following definition of leadership:

> Leadership is the ability to accurately understand the present and significantly impact the future.

In addition, as a result of our extensive experience in helping schools improve teaching and learning, we have come to recognize this important "truth" about leadership:

Not every individual in a successful organization has the ability to be an effective leader, but successful organizations have effective leaders at every level within the organization.

This "truth" indicates how essential it is for the principal to develop faculty leaders who have the ability and the commitment to share the responsibility of facilitating the CIS. No system can be successful if the principal is the only person leading the implementation process. Successful implementation requires direct involvement of both the principal and faculty members. In every single experience we have had with the implementation of the CIS in a school, there was one constant, and that was the direct correlation of the principal's leadership with the level of success.

The leadership ability and the passion demonstrated by the principal are the primary determinants of how successfully the System will be implemented.

Marzano, Waters, and McNulty (2005) have provided some very helpful information about principal leadership in their book, *School Leadership That Works*. They identified 21 leadership responsibilities that significantly impacted student achievement. In a following paper, "Balanced leadership: what 30 years of research tells us about the effect of leadership on student achievement," they explained the correlation as follows: "Consider schools A and B with similar student and teacher populations. Both schools demonstrate student achievement on standardized, norm-referenced tests at the fiftieth percentile. Principals of both schools are ranked at the fiftieth percentile in their abilities on the 21 leadership responsibilities. If Principal B improves his abilities in each of the leadership responsibilities by one standard deviation, our research indicates that this increase translates into student achievement in school B rising 10 percentile points over student achievement in school A."

We compared Marzano, Waters, and McNulty's list of 21 leadership responsibilities with the requirements of the principal while implementing the CIS and found several definite connections, especially with the seven responsibilities that those authors cited as most positively impacting second-order change.

When a leader facilitates changes in the minor functions of an organization and these can be done with current knowledge and resources, it is first-order change. However, if the changes significantly alter how individuals in the organization do their core work and this new work requires new knowledge and a redistribution of resources, it is second-order change. Because the Continuous Improvement System is most definitely second-order change, we wanted to see how it fit with the research of Marzano, Waters, and McNulty. Table 4.1 depicts the activities of the principal in the Continuous Improvement System and the responsibilities of the principal that impact second-order change as identified by Marzano, Waters, and McNulty.

Table 4.1. Comparison of the Responsibilities of the Principal

Continuous Improvement System	Leadership That Works
Being knowledgeable about instructional calendars, common assessments, data collection, data charts—facilitating data dialogue by instructional teams, focused on improving teacher practice and student achievement	Knowledge of Curriculum, Instruction, and Assessment—being knowledgeable about how the innovation will affect curricular, instructional, and assessment practices and providing conceptual guidance in these areas
Being the guardian of the school vision, academic mission, core commitments—stressing high expectations through continuous improvement dialogue	Optimizer—being the driving force behind the new innovation and fostering the belief that it can produce exceptional results if members of the staff are willing to apply themselves
Being a planner and presenter of professional development identified by real-time data with a focus on improving instruction and generating ways of assisting struggling students	Intellectual Stimulation—being knowledgeable about the research and theory regarding the innovation and fostering such knowledge among staff through reading and discussion
Using real-time data to challenge current practices—acting as the facilitator of work accomplished by instructional teams and the leadership team	Change Agent—challenging the status quo and being willing to move forward on the innovation without a guarantee of success
Monitoring real-time data generated by classroom- and grade-level charts—frequently observing classroom instruction and conducting post-observation coaching	Monitoring/Evaluating—continually monitoring the impact of the innovation
Facilitating leadership team, instructional team, and faculty meetings—acting as both a teacher and co-learner of new practices	Flexibility—being both directive and nondirective relative to the innovation as the situation warrants
Displaying confidence in and a commitment to the Continuous Improvement System—living the belief that the faculty and the students can achieve the goals of the System	Ideas/Beliefs—operating in a manner consistent with his ideals and beliefs relative to the innovation

Source: Adapted with permission of McREL.

THE ROLE OF DIALOGUE

In later chapters, you will learn about the documents used within the Continuous Improvement System and the specific purpose of each document. Each document is necessary and helpful, but it is important to remember that they are just documents. The real power of the documents is in the dialogue that occurs as administrators and teachers create and use them. Dialogue is a team learning activity that requires a variety of communication skills to be effective.

The term *dialogue* in the CIS refers to the free flow of ideas that occurs when people truly think together in an open, honest, and respectful manner. The purpose of dialogue is to explore everyone's thoughts and feelings about any given topic. It provides all faculty members with the opportunity to influence how issues are addressed.

Dialogue requires that people examine their personal mental models and then suspend their assumptions and personal biases as they consider multiple options that potentially will achieve a desired result. This is easy to say and difficult to do. As human beings, we cannot avoid making assumptions. As Peter Senge states in *The Fifth Discipline* (1990), "We are simply wired that way."

Since it is virtually impossible for individuals not to have assumptions about a change that will impact them, it is important to name and sort these assumptions. Once this is done, someone with knowledge about the proposed change can talk directly with individuals or the faculty as a group and provide valuable factual information that either affirms the assumption as true or invalidates it. This process of openly addressing assumptions typically lowers resistance to the change and increases trust among administrators and faculty members. The Assumption Sort and Inventory activity helps team members name and address these inevitable assumptions. This tool is provided in the Communication section of the appendix.

Another common communication problem that can interfere with effective dialogue is the tendency to mix up thoughts and feelings. They are very distinct items in a dialogue and the more capable team members are in differentiating between them, the more effective and productive are their dialogues. Unexpressed or misunderstood feelings can result in dysfunctional teamwork with some or many members taking a reactive rather than a proactive approach to working on the change being implemented.

Inviting team members to intentionally name both their thoughts and their feelings about a proposed change from time to time can help people communicate more authentically and stay more proactive as they work to implement the change. The Communication section of the appendix has a tool that helps team members become more skilled in clearly sharing their thoughts and feelings as they respond to the thoughts and feelings of others.

We stress again that dialogue is a powerful antidote to the professional isolation that often occurs in schools. *We believe that the quality of this dialogue is the single most critical factor in the transformation of the culture of the school.* We have repeatedly observed that the better the dialogue skills of team members in a school, the faster and more effectively the System works. Consequently one of the principal's key responsibilities is to model, support, and nurture the development of dialogue skills. Every faculty member must be skilled in using dialogue as a communication tool with colleagues.

THE ROLE OF ADVOCACY

Groups often splinter and become ineffective because some or all members of the group enter meetings with the intent of presenting and defending their personal idea. This behavior of personal advocacy focuses on one idea being strongly presented and it severely diminishes the opportunity for exploration of other options. If a strong advocacy pattern continues over time, 80 percent of the influence during a meeting designed to determine what action the team will take will come from 20 percent of the team's members. This is an example of the well-known Pareto Principle. This pattern of team interaction results in wasted time and minimal ownership of the product of the meeting.

On the other hand, team learning through the process of dialogue makes it possible to raise a group's collective knowledge to a level above that of any single member of the group. Dialogue results in more and better options and more effective solutions than any single member of the group can produce alone. Dialogue does not produce winners and losers. Instead, it leads people down a path toward authentic consensus decision making.

This is not to say that advocacy does not have a place in team communication. It does, but the timing of its use is important. It should occur after the group has engaged in an appropriate amount of dialogue and narrowed the possible targeted results to a limited number of plausible options. At this point, individuals can advocate for what they believe is the best course of action. Advocacy can produce a winning option that all of the team members can support when used in the proper sequence with dialogue. Advocating for an option might sound like this:

The facilitator of the meeting says, "We are finished with our dialogue about adjusting the schedule for our instructional team meetings. We have explored a variety of options and thanks to our focused conversations we have generated three possibilities. We have posted these options on the flip chart. Look at them, choose the one you think best fits our needs, and be prepared to explain your decision."

The facilitator then calls on a variety of people and the advocacy comments are recorded in a location where everyone can see them. If time allows, there could be some question-and-answer opportunities following the advocacy exercise. If there is not enough time, this Q and A can be done via e-mail.

Once the facilitator determines that there has been sufficient opportunity for advocacy, he calls for a decision. This could be done in a variety of ways.

- Faculty members go to their option of choice on the wall and the one with the most people is the schedule for the rest of the school year.
- They do a hand vote.
- They do a paper ballot vote.

As the culture of the full faculty team changes over time and trust grows, there is less and less need for secret paper ballots. However, in the beginning they may be needed.

MEETING SKILLS FOR EDUCATIONAL PROFESSIONALS

The CSI is implemented in two different arenas. One is in the classroom and the other is in meetings. Both are equally important. The classroom is the arena in which the teacher has the opportunity to apply the CIS with students. The meeting is the arena in which the teacher has the opportunity to work collaboratively with colleagues to plan what they want to happen in the classroom.

However, planning and facilitating effective meetings requires considerable skill. Unfortunately, this is a skill set that many educators lack. Conducting effective meetings has not been a part of the teacher or administrator preparation curriculum in the universities. The result is that educators often enter meetings without a clear focus and exit without a clear direction. Faculty members generally do not look at faculty meetings as an opportunity. Meetings are considered to be more of an obligation and as a result waste huge amounts of time and resources. To calculate the cost of such a meeting, multiply the number of people involved in the meeting by the average hourly wage of these people. The total makes a strong case for learning and using the meeting skills of planning and facilitation.

Effective meetings are essential for the successful implementation of the CIS. These meetings provide time and opportunity for the dialogue, and consequently, they must be well planned and effectively facilitated. This requires a set of skills that includes:

- Developing and following meeting norms that ensure respectful communication and interaction
- Planning an agenda
- Ensuring clarity about whether the purpose of an agenda item is dialogue about an item or the opportunity for advocacy for a specific option relating to that item
- Maintaining succinct and accurate minutes of the meeting
- Maintaining a record of decisions made during a meeting
- Identifying who will lead the implementation of each decision and the timeline for the implementation
- Maintaining a success file

The success file is a collection of materials and instructional strategies that have proven to be effective. It also includes adjustments to the time that must be scheduled on an instructional calendar for a particular unit and notes on practical organizational practices. The success file provides a designated place to keep ideas that will enhance future instruction and aid in planning instructional units. This file becomes a powerful set of materials to offer to new teachers and substitute teachers. It plays an important role in developing a culture of professionalism and collaboration. You will see this "success file" mentioned again as a part of the agenda for meetings in chapter 5 as a part of the Instructional Team Data–Dialogue Meeting Agenda.

The Meeting Room

If at all possible, the principal should designate a single room for all instructional team and leadership team meetings. The room must afford team members with ample table space and comfortable seating. The following items should be clearly displayed in the room:

1. The school vision, academic mission, core commitments, and meeting norms
2. The grade-level/subject instructional calendars and data charts
3. Other pertinent data concerning student achievement such as:

- High-stakes test data from the state
- District quarterly test data
- Other ongoing data such as reading data

4. Three-ring binders for each grade level/subject to organize such things as:

- State standards
- District curriculum maps/pacing guides
- Meeting schedules and agendas

- Meeting minutes
- Success files
- Instructional calendars (blank forms)
- Sources for common assessment items
- Data collection and error analysis forms

5. A computer that allows access to the Internet and a printer. This is a very valuable tool as teachers search for new instructional strategies, materials, and test item banks, and for recording meeting minutes.

The items must communicate the message that this room is a place where professional and collaborative work is done. Any person who enters this room should understand this message as soon as he walks in the door.

TIME ISSUES

It is the responsibility of the principal to provide time for the work to be done. Even though he cannot create more hours in the day, he can carefully choose how to spend the time that is available. It is a matter of establishing agreed-upon priorities. He must learn to schedule priorities rather than prioritize the schedule. Here are some ideas that will help with this challenge.

The principal must become skilled at communicating most of the managerial "stuff" that teachers need to know through group e-mail or a weekly newsletter. In addition teachers must accept the responsibility for reading these documents and be held accountable for doing so as well as completing any assignments communicated in this way.

We strongly suggest that every attempt be made to provide common planning time within the master class schedule for teachers who teach the same grade or subject. This time must be protected and devoted to instructional team activities and individual teacher preparation. If teachers are provided with such time, they will produce instructional calendars, common assessments, and instructional materials that are of higher quality than if they are left to create these essential items individually and on their own time.

Some schools, due to their size and other conflicts, are unable to provide common time within the master schedule. When this is the case, the leadership team needs to work to develop a creative solution. This common time to work with colleagues is essential if the CIS is going to operate at an optimal level.

To facilitate collaboration and make instructional team meetings easier to organize, we suggest that the rooms of teachers who teach the same grade level/subject be located in close proximity. This will encourage both formal and informal communication between and among these teachers. This is

A TIME STORY

The principal and the leadership team knew that the current master schedule would not provide the time necessary for instructional teams to meet and turned to a creative solution.

By contract, the teachers were required to be on duty 20 minutes prior to the time that students enter the classroom. The school devotes the first 25 minutes of the first class period to a Breakfast in the Classroom program. As that program was originally conceived, teachers supervised students in their own classrooms. By moving the program to the cafeteria and utilizing special-area teachers and other nonclassroom teacher personnel to supervise, a common planning time of 45 minutes was created. Instructional team meetings are now scheduled during this time and staggered throughout the week, making it possible for the principal to attend the meeting of each grade level. When the teams are not formally engaged in a meeting, they use the time to supplement the individual planning time that was built into the master schedule. The teachers viewed this adjustment as strong support from the school's leadership that was clearly intended to help them meet the expectations of the principal.

especially valuable in schools that are departmentalized and have teachers who teach two subjects. If two teachers teach both algebra and geometry, each must choose a primary instructional team. The close location of their classrooms would allow them to communicate about the work of both instructional teams.

The district can also support the implementation of the System at the school level by scheduling early release days that are devoted to instructional team and professional development activities. It is important to have the priority of common planning time clearly and consistently supported by the superintendent and other appropriate district-level personnel. When this support comes from the top of the authority chain, it is much more likely that the time will be scheduled and used for the designated purpose of instructional team activities and individual teacher preparation.

Individual Teacher Time

We are often asked the very legitimate question, "How much additional teacher time does this System take?" The answer is very little. The System does not ask anything of teachers that they do not already do or should do. Instead the System changes how and with whom they do things. For example:

- *Teachers already plan instruction.* Instructional planning in the CIS is done through the instructional calendar. This will initially take a small amount of additional time as the teachers learn the process. However, this more organized approach to scheduling the content will, in time, give teachers ample time for collaboratively developing their instructional calendars once a month. In our experience with the System, we find that teachers working collectively make better decisions about what content is critical to teach and what content is optional.
- *Teachers already develop tests.* The CIS simply requires that the test be written in a specific format. Because the teachers work together to simultaneously develop both formative tests and tests that are used in the teach/reteach sequence, no additional time is required. Again, we have found they develop better assessments when they are working together.
- *Teachers already grade the tests and record the scores.* The only additional time required in the System comes from determining the percentage of students who met or exceeded the academic mission and using a colored highlighter to enter the data on the classroom data chart. This may take approximately two minutes.
- *Teachers should already be carefully evaluating the types and causes of student errors.* Again, when they can do this in a collaborative effort, they can help each other be more objective and more accurate.
- *Teachers should be engaging in and learning new and effective practices.* Teachers become teachers of each other when they discuss strategies that worked in a classroom. They become mutual problem solvers when they discuss a strategy that did not work in a classroom.

The Continuous Improvement System is based on teachers working in teams. Initially, scheduling this time can seem difficult. However, as soon as teachers discover that truly, "More heads are better than one!" they will find ways to schedule that collaborative time. As they partner with each other, with the principal, and with the students, they not only find creative ways to schedule time, but also they use the time more effectively. In our experience the change from the attitude of "There is no way we can find time to do that much collaboration" to "I could not survive without our collaboration time" is five months or less.

Chapter Five

Collaboration

THE TEAMS DOING THE WORK

According to noted American psychologist Dr. William Glasser, our behavior is driven by a minimal number of basic human needs. A desire to belong, to be accepted by others, is one of those needs. In his article, "The Quality School" (1990), he concludes that "Learning together as a member of a team satisfies the need to belong much better than does learning alone." Because we know this to be true, we have designed the Continuous Improvement System around teams of people working in collaboration. The idea of teams of people working in collaboration in education is not new. In the past 10 years there has been a deluge of programs, ideas, and suggestions for helping teachers and administrators work together in collaborative learning teams. What is different about the CIS is what the teachers do in these teams.

The Continuous Improvement System requires three different teams with each having a distinct purpose. All three are required for the CIS to function at the optimal level. They are:

1) The instructional teams at each grade level or content area
2) The leadership team
3) The faculty as a whole

Each of these teams meet on a regular basis and work from well-planned agendas designed to make the maximum use of time and the talents of the members of the teams.

WHAT DOES THE INSTRUCTIONAL TEAM DO?

Education Week, June 2010, volume 36, issue 29, the 2009 Metlife Survey of the American Teacher. This survey concluded that "Today's teachers work alone—they spend an average of 93 percent of their time working in isolation from their colleagues. Their day-to-day work is disconnected from the efforts of their colleagues. They continue to work alone during their out-of-school hours of preparation and grading. Their work is disconnected from the efforts of their colleagues. Their pullout professional development is fragmented and poorly aligned with their students' learning needs."

This information is very troublesome in light of all the recent focus on the importance of teachers working together in professional learning communities. Because it is clear that the challenges facing educators today cannot be solved when teachers are working in isolation, the CIS requires that teachers work in job-alike, collaborative teams.

Instructional teams are comprised of the teachers from a given grade level or teachers who teach a common subject. Participation in an instructional team is not optional. Every faculty member is on such a team.

Every instructional team has a facilitator who presides over the meetings. This person may or may not be a teacher in the grade level or subject area. For instance, an instructional team facilitator could be an administrator, an instructional coach, or a special-area teacher. Finding someone who can command the respect of his colleagues is the key criterion for selecting a facilitator. This person also represents their instructional team as a member of the leadership team.

The benefit of having grade-level or department chairpersons serve in this role is that they have firsthand knowledge of the subject matter. On the other hand, the benefit of having someone like an assistant principal or curriculum coordinator in this role is the ease of arranging leadership team meetings without the need for substitute teachers. Also, having someone from the "outside" as facilitator can help avoid jealousy and potential conflict within the instructional team. Such a person is also in a better position to hold the teachers accountable for their actions.

The instructional teams meet on a regular basis. Through trial-and-error scheduling, we have found it works best to hold one meeting near the end of each month to prepare the instructional calendar (see chapter 7) and the common assessments (see chapter 9) for the following month. In addition, following each formative assessment the instructional teams meet to engage in a data-and-dialogue session. This gives teachers the opportunity to individually and collectively review the data, determine student progress, and plan instructional strategies to use as they teach or reteach a lesson.

Initially, the dialogue in these meetings may be an uncomfortable experience for many teachers because the agenda makes public the formative assessment data from each teacher's classroom. It is very clear whose students succeeded and whose did not. As a result, each teacher becomes fully aware of how students are performing in their colleagues' classrooms. Despite this initial discomfort, teachers soon discover the power of dialoguing with their colleagues about student performance data. When they do, the levels of trust and collaboration increase within the instructional team.

There is also an interesting system-level impact that occurs. As teachers discover the powerful impact of dialogue in instructional teams, the levels of trust and collaboration across the school will increase. Over time, the culture of the school changes from one of private practice to one of public and collegial practice.

The facilitator of the instructional team plays a pivotal role in the transformation of the culture by guarding against competition between or among team members. The facilitator must make it clear that the purpose of the instructional team is to ensure that the learning of every student improves, not to identify one teacher as the winner because he has the highest formative assessment scores. The facilitator conducts meetings in a manner that allows teachers to gain insight into students' individual and collective needs, and to develop instructional practices that will more effectively meet those needs. He also encourages teachers to help one another adjust their instructional practices when data indicate that a change is needed.

Weinstein (1991) addresses the shift from the competitive phenomenon in her study on collaborative school change. She observed that, "initially, participating teachers brought to the group an atmosphere of competition. Over time, the atmosphere changed to one of collaborative analysis and scrutiny of teaching practices. This produced a climate of mutual trust and respect."

As we mentioned previously, all three teams work from well-planned agendas when they gather in meetings. The instructional team meetings are guided by two different agendas. The first is for a content planning meeting in which teachers identify and sequence the curriculum for the next month. The second is for a data–dialogue meeting in which teachers analyze data from formative assessments and use the data to adjust their instruction and better meet student needs. Because the actual format of the agendas is not critical, a school may choose to create any format that meets the unique needs of the school. However, it is important to include the major components cited in the example agendas that follow.

INSTRUCTIONAL TEAM

PLANNING MEETING AGENDA

Planning Meeting (The curriculum content for the next month)

A. Review Meeting Norms (These are explained in chapter 6.)

B. The Instructional Calendar (This is explained in chapter 7.)

  1. Select and schedule the priority performance objectives
  2. Ensure a common understanding by all teachers of what each performance objective is asking students to know and be able to do after instruction

C. The Formative Assessment

  1. Create two parallel forms of the common assessment (This is explained in chapter 9.)
     • Match the content, language, format, and rigor of the items to the objective(s) and the high-stakes test
     • Group the items and identify them by the performance objective they measure
  2. Enter the assessment on the classroom and grade-level/subject data charts (These are explained in chapter 10.)

D. The Instructional Strategies

  1. Review instructional strategies and materials that have been effective in the past
  2. Determine how these and/or new strategies will be used
  3. Determine how these and/or new materials will be used

E. Develop an action plan designating who will do what and by when

It is essential that teachers pay careful attention to item C.1 in the agenda. This emphasizes the need to create formative assessments that accurately measure the performance objectives and prepare students for the high-stakes test.

The first bullet in agenda item C.1 directs the teachers to:

1. Ensure that the *content* of the formative assessment matches the content of the performance objective. The formative assessment item must require the student to demonstrate the specific knowledge or skill that is identified in the performance objective. Nothing more and nothing less.
2. Ensure that the *language* used to state the performance objective matches the language the student will hear during instruction and see on the formative assessment and the high-stakes test.
3. Ensure that the appearance or *format* of the formative assessment matches what the student will see on the high-stakes test.
4. Ensure that the level of difficulty or *rigor* of the formative assessment matches what the student will experience on the high-stakes test.

Teachers who use this four-point test to construct their formative assessments will find that their students will be better prepared for the high-stakes test.

To demonstrate the critical nature of this activity, consider the story of the Avid Golfer (AG). Because AG felt that he could significantly lower his handicap by improving his putting skill, he spent hours on the practice green stroking 3-foot, flat, straight putts. When he was able to consistently make 98 of 100 of these putts, he concluded that he was now a much better putter. However, when he played on the golf course, on the first hole he faced a 10-foot, downhill, left-to-right breaking putt. He badly missed the putt. This outcome was predictable because the data that he used to conclude that he was a skilled putter was faulty. The method that he used to collect the data was fatally flawed. The skill that AG practiced was not a match for the skill that he needed on the golf course.

If we apply the four-point test to this scenario, we quickly understand AG's error.

1. Did the *content* of AG's practice match the actual activity on the golf course? In this story, the answer is a qualified yes. Both are associated with the game of golf and the specific skill of putting.
2. Did the *language* of the practice activity match the language of the experience on the golf course? The answer is no. In no way do the descriptive words of 3-feet, flat, and straight found in the practice activity match the descriptive words of 10-feet, downhill, and left-to-right break of the on-course experience.
3. Did the *format* of the practice green match the format of the on-course green? The answer is no. What AG saw and experienced on the practice green was not a match for what he saw and experienced on the course.
4. Did the *rigor* of the practice putts match the rigor of the on-course putt? The answer is no. The degree of difficulty in making a 10-foot, downhill, left-to-right breaking putt is much higher than that of making a 3-foot, flat, straight putt.

If the answer to one or more of the questions associated with the four-point test is no, the formative assessment must be reconsidered and brought into line with the high-stakes test.

If the four-point test is applied to a mathematics example we may find a situation in which a teacher reads a performance objective that states, "The student will use the skill of adding two-digit numbers with regrouping to solve real life problems" and then writes a formative assessment item that says, "Add 19 and 17." This item clearly fails the four-point test and will not prepare the student for a high-stakes test. A better question might be: "John and Joe want to buy a football that costs $34. John has saved $19 and Joe has saved $17. If they add their savings together, do they have enough money to buy the football?"

Unless the four-point test is used in the construction of formative assessments, teachers run the risk of creating flawed assessments that may lead to inflated student achievement scores. Conclusions about the students' level of preparation for a high-stakes test based on such data can only lead to disappointment when the high-stakes test results are posted.

When producing formative assessments, teachers must remember that you cannot prepare someone to successfully make 10-foot, downhill, left-to-right breaking putts by having the person practice 3-foot, flat, straight putts.

INSTRUCTIONAL TEAM
DATA-DIALOGUE MEETING AGENDA
A COLLABORATIVE EFFORT

Data-Dialogue Meeting **(The data from the most recent assessment)**

A. Review Meeting Norms (These are explained in chapter 6.)

B. Data Analysis and Dialogue
    1. Review Classroom Data Charts

    • Which objectives were most difficult for students?
    • What errors did students make? Review the Error Analysis From (This is explained in chapter 9.)
    • What are the underlying causes of the errors?
    • What instructional strategies and materials were/were not effective?
    • What will be said to students when the assessment is returned?
    • Which students did/did not meet the academic mission and how will their needs be addressed? (The academic mission is explained in chapter 6.)
    • How will this data be used to better prepare students for the next assessment?

C. Grade-level/Subject Chart
    1. Record the classroom data on the Grade-level/Subject Chart (This is explained in chapter 10.)

D. Success File
    1. Place effective strategies and materials in a success file for future reference

E. Develop an action plan designating who will do what and by when

---

WHAT DOES THE LEADERSHIP TEAM DO?

The leadership team is comprised of administrators, the facilitators of the instructional teams, and any other personnel that the principal thinks would add to the quality functioning of the team. The people on this team must be trusted and highly respected by both the principal and the faculty as a whole. The level of commitment and skill this team exhibits has a direct correlation to the success of CIS in the school.

The CIS provides a structure and process for school leaders to use as they work to answer this call. In the System the leadership team is responsible for ensuring that instructional teams follow the principles that the NCTAF found to be common to highly effective teacher teams. These principles are:

- Team members must have a common vision of student learning needs and how their collective capabilities can be utilized to meet those needs.
- Team members function in roles that make optimal use of their knowledge and experience. They see themselves as mutually responsible for success and collectively accountable for improving student achievement.
- Team members use common assessments that provide real-time feedback on student achievement and use the data to improve the team's effectiveness. They establish a reflective feedback loop of data analysis, planning, and goal setting.

LEADERSHIP TEAM
MEETING AGENDA
A COLLABORATIVE EFFORT

A. Review Meeting Norms (These are explained in chapter 6.)

B. Prior Actions
1. Review the actions that were taken to address areas of concern identified during previous meetings
2. Determine the effectiveness of the actions and identify any additional action that is necessary

C. Current Student Achievement Data
1. Review the Grade-level/Subject Data Charts (These are explained in chapter 10.)
2. Review the individual teacher data from the Data Collection Forms (These are explained in chapter 10.)
3. Analyze the impact of the reteach/retest process
4. What actions are necessary to address areas of concern or celebrate successes

D. Faculty Meeting
1. Plan the vision, mission, commitments, or rules activity (These are explained in chapter 6.)
2. Plan the Data-Dialogue Activity
   - Determine if this will be a whole group activity or an instructional team activity
   - Plan the report to the whole faculty and feedback activity
3. Plan the Professional Development activity
4. Plan the Nonteaching/Learning Items
   - Correlate Team (committee) Reports
   - District Information
   - Other Pertinent Information

E. Develop an action plan designating who will do what and by when

The leadership team meets on a regular basis with a schedule of one meeting every two weeks being optimal. As with the instructional teams, a well-planned agenda ensures that the desired work is accomplished. Items about instructional leadership are always first on the agenda because this sends a clear message that teaching and learning are the top priorities.

All leadership team agendas should include the major components depicted in the example agenda that follows.

WHAT DOES THE FACULTY DO?

Timely, accurate, and clear communication among all faculty members is a critical part of the Continuous Improvement System because the decisions made by instructional teams and the leadership team can only be effectively implemented if the entire faculty is informed and has some ownership in those decisions. Communication happens best in well-planned faculty meetings. Here again, the major focus is always on teaching and learning. When meetings are well planned and all members skillfully participate, the entire faculty participates in the creation of a collaborative and professional culture. As a result faculty members begin to look forward to this opportunity to work with their colleagues across subjects and grade levels.

What is the Role of Professional Development during a Faculty Meeting?

The professional development activity part of the faculty meeting agenda should meet a three-pronged test.

1. The professional development topic is internally identified.
2. The training is embedded and ongoing.
3. People are held accountable for utilizing the newly acquired skills.

The content of the professional development can be identified through the dialogue that occurs in any of the three team meetings previously described. A need for some specific type of professional development may also become apparent as administrators observe classrooms. The bottom line is the faculty must see and agree with the need for the development of new skills because imposing professional development upon the adult learner is rarely, if ever, effective.

The training should be done at the school and span a period of time that is sufficient to allow staff members to gain a clear understanding of the content and allow ample time to practice the new skill. In addition, every effort should be made to link this learning with the learning of previous staff development sessions. When these connections are clear, staff members are more likely to build a systems approach to improving their practice.

Achieving higher levels of student engagement is the immediate or eventual desired outcome of the vast majority of professional development for teachers and administrators. It will require more than a few sessions to effectively explore and master new instructional strategies that will accomplish this. If teachers are going to use a strategy with fidelity, they must have ample opportunity to gain a clear insight into what the students will experience when they use the strategy in the classroom. They need a chance to collaboratively plan, experiment, and critique the results of a new strategy with colleagues.

FACULTY MEETING AGENDA
A COLLABORATIVE EFFORT

A. Review Meeting Norms (These are explained in chapter 6.)

B. Celebration of Success

C. Vision, Mission, Commitments, or Rules Activity (These are explained in chapter 6.)

D. Data-Dialogue
   a. Review grade-level/subject reports and/or district quartely test reports

   • Celebrate areas of success
   • Identify areas needing attention
   • Does the area needing attention appear in prior/future curriculum
   • What is the level of student preparedness as they enter each grade
   • What must be done to ensure students' success at each level
   • Are there other grade-level/subject articulation issues
   • Suggestions for instructional strategies and materials
   • Which students did/did not meet the academic mission and how will their needs be addressed (The academic mission is explained in chapter 6.)

E. Professional Development Activity

F. Nonteaching/Learning Items
   1. Correlate Team (committee) Reports
   2. District Information
   3. Other Pertinent Information

G. Develop an action plan designating who will do what and by when

The administrators in the school must make it explicitly clear that they will expect to see the newly acquired strategies being used when they visit classrooms. The teacher evaluation system can be used to formally hold people accountable for applying what they are learning. However, this needs to be done in a way that helps teachers learn from their mistakes and celebrates their progress in improving their teaching practice.

The administrator also must "walk the talk" of the professional development. One way to accomplish this is for the administrator to model and label the skills he and the faculty recently learned in the professional development activities as he facilitates faculty meetings. At the end of the meeting he can ask for feedback concerning what he did well and for some suggestions for improvement.

Another way is for the administrator to model the skills in a classroom. He teaches a lesson or a part of the lesson and intentionally uses the strategy. Later he discusses the results with the teacher, again asking for feedback and exploring ways that the teacher can use the skill. This is instructional leadership in action.

Chapter Six

Developing the Key Documents

GETTING EVERYONE ON THE SAME PAGE

Have you ever been a member of a group that "just clicked"? If so, did you find that the group consisted of people that you both liked and respected? Did you become aware that when you were apart, you began to look forward to being together again? Did you feel that each member of the group was excited by the pursuit of a common goal? Were you proud of the fact that the members of the group were brave enough to encourage the free flow of ideas and cohesive enough to debate the merits of those ideas without damaging the relationships?

If you have enjoyed an experience like the one described above, you are fortunate indeed, because such groups are not common. Many people go through their entire lives without this experience. If you are now part of a group where these characteristics exist, protect it fiercely. If you are part of a group that is beginning to develop these characteristics, intentionally and carefully nurture that development. If you are part of a group that is far from the ideal, the good news is that it is possible to engineer a culture in which these desirable group characteristics can emerge and thrive. It is possible to "get everyone on the same page."

Various researchers have expressed this concept in a variety of ways. In the original Effective Schools research, Edmonds, Brookover, and Lezotte found that schools demonstrating high levels of student achievement shared a "clear and focused mission." Dr. Peter Senge, in *The Fifth Discipline,* writes about a "shared vision." When this vision and mission are in place people within an effective organization know, understand, and willingly pursue the ultimate goal of the organization.

41

When a leader chooses to implement the Continuous Improvement System, the following key documents provide the blueprint for bringing this important "same page" concept to life. These documents help the leader involve the team members in designing a preferred future for the team, setting targeted improvements that the team strives to realize and making clear commitments to working together to successfully make those improvements.

These documents are:

- A School Vision Statement—a statement of how the faculty wants the school to function
- An Academic Mission Statement—a clear statement of the student achievement target
- A Core Commitments Statement—a statement of the behaviors that the faculty agrees to exhibit as they pursue the school vision and the academic mission
- A set of Meeting Norms—a description of how faculty members will respectfully treat each other in meetings
- A set of School Rules—a list of agreed-upon behaviors for students and faculty

We order the documents in this sequence because the school vision is the big picture; the academic mission is the major move the team takes in order to make that big picture a reality; and the remaining documents describe how they will behave as they work together. The sequence goes from a shared big picture to specific behaviors. However, that is not the order of creating the documents. In the remainder of this chapter we explain each document in detail and note the order in which they should be developed.

THE SCHOOL VISION

An effective leader knows that a shared vision cannot be forced; it must be cultivated and nurtured. He knows how to create the conditions for developing a shared vision that actually drives the work of the organization. He knows how to model the concepts and the skills necessary to achieve a shared vision. He clearly communicates his expectations about the vision and provides the support necessary for people to meet those expectations.

Although it may seem logical to write this document first, we suggest that it be the last one that the faculty writes. The school vision is a document that is philosophical in nature while the other four documents are much more concrete. Writing the other four first helps shape the image to be portrayed in the school vision.

The school vision is a statement that creates an image of the organization that people aspire to create. Another descriptor of the school vision is "our desired future." Often such a statement contains words and terms that are not measurable. They describe students as "lifelong learners" and "productive adult citizens." Teachers may never know if their students go on to become productive adults, but inspiring students to do so is an important part of a teacher's work.

The No Child Left Behind legislation calls for all students to perform at grade level. This is a wonderful vision, but honest educators will state that it is an unattainable target. Some students simply do not have the mental capacity to achieve the desired level of performance. It is more realistic for educators to be challenged to take all children to the highest level that their ability allows, even if it is not to the grade level commensurate with their chronological age. And yet the reality of the second statement should not deter us from pursuing the vision in the first place because the pursuit of the unattainable is often a powerful catalyst for improving performance.

The game of golf provides a good example of pursuing the unattainable. This is true whether you are just learning how to play or if you are trying to improve your game. Golf pros often say, "Don't move your head." This is a poor teaching direction because it is stated in the negative. It is impossible to not do something. You must do something! A better direction is "See the club head strike the ball." Of course the speed of the action makes it impossible for you to do this, but the attempt will make you keep your head still and improve your swing. It helps you picture the right thing to do. That is what a good vision statement does.

Here is an example of a school vision.

We, the educators of _____ School, ensure that our students will become lifelong learners and productive members of the adult society. This is accomplished in a challenging but caring environment through the combined efforts of a dedicated faculty.

During the first days of our work with a school, we intentionally visit many classrooms with the purpose of determining whether or not a vision statement is "alive and well," and actually driving the work. When we ask the educators who work in the building what that document says, the answers range from, "Oh, that. We spent hours writing it. What a waste of time" to "I don't know. I think that it says something about lifelong learners." These responses clearly indicate that the statement is not a driving force in the school. Instead, we can safely conclude that the faculty wrote it to simply fulfill a requirement at some point in the past.

There are three reliable indicators of an effective vision. First, an effective school vision is a brief statement of no more than two sentences that *everyone* knows and understands. All the educators in the school are proud of the statement and can clearly explain both the words and the spirit of the document. Second, all faculty members have been involved in creating the statement. Despite the fact that writing by committee is a challenge, it is critical that the faculty reaches consensus on the language in this document. Third, the vision is often a topic of discussion. The faculty should frequently ask and answer the question, "Does this project fit our school vision?"

Writing a school vision statement takes time, flexibility, and honest dialogue. We offer the following process to assist you in meeting the challenge of creating a meaningful statement that truly guides the work of the school.

Process for Creating the School Vision

1. Determine who will facilitate the process. It is an effective practice to have the principal act as the overall facilitator and assign members of the implementation team to work with the small work groups.
2. Seat the faculty in small work groups. The membership of each group should be no less than five and no more than eight.
3. Provide each group with markers, flip chart paper, and tape.
4. Select a recorder/reporter for the group and provide appropriate materials.
5. Explain to the group that this is a collaborative effort. From this point on, it is important to focus on ownership of the end product as opposed to ownership of the work created by any individual group.
6. Ask each group to identify a list of words or phrases that depict its vision of the school.
7. Ask one group to report its list and post it in a location that is visible to the entire faculty. Continue the process by asking each group to add, from its list, any words or phrases that do not already appear. This will result in a lengthy list of words and phrases.
8. Ask each group to consider the entire list and select five words or phrases that are *most* important to them.
9. Ask one group to report and record its revised list of five words or phrases. Continue the process by asking each group to add, from its list, any words or phrases that do not already appear. This "narrowing" process will result in some words and phrases being eliminated. Repeat this process until consensus (a minimum of 80 percent agreement) is reached on four or five words or phrases. It is important to limit the list in order to write a clear and concise statement.

10. Ask each group to use the agreed-upon words or phrases to develop two clearly worded sentences as the initial draft of the school vision statement.
11. Repeat steps 6–10 that were used to identify the words or phrases to help the group reach consensus on a vision statement that will drive their work.

Writing a school vision statement requires time, patience, and persistence. It may take several meetings to allow people sufficient time to thoughtfully reflect on the document and become comfortable with the language. The process may require some individuals to let go of their personal favorite word or phrase. When this happens the principal must take the time to talk to these individuals to ensure that they are comfortable with their sacrifice and can support the final document. Doing so makes it much less likely that they will overtly or covertly harbor hurt feelings that might eventually lead to their diminished efforts or, worse, to one or more of these individuals becoming an undermining force within the group.

THE ACADEMIC MISSION—FORMATIVE AND SUMMATIVE VERSIONS

The academic mission is a specific statement about the desired level of academic achievement. It should be the first of the key documents that the faculty writes. The term "mission" refers to the Effective Schools "clear and focused mission" correlate and is used in the military sense. For instance, when a team of Navy Seals is sent on a mission, they know exactly what they are to accomplish and how success will be measured. When the faculty has written the academic mission, they will know exactly what they are to accomplish and how they will measure their success.

Faculty members will actually write two versions of the academic mission. One expresses a summative goal for student achievement that sets the standard for student performance on the high-stakes test that occurs near the end of the school year. The second version of the academic mission expresses a formative goal. It sets the standard for student performance throughout the school year.

The reason the faculty must write these two statements is because they use both formative and summative data as they assess student progress. Summative data, such as the data generated by end-of-year high-stakes tests, can be very useful in identifying trends in the achievement levels of previous students. However, these data are not helpful to the individual teacher as he monitors the ongoing academic achievement of the students who are now in his classroom. Such monitoring requires formative data. Real-time, formative data provides the teacher with the information needed to monitor student performance and adjust the instructional strategies in order to effectively address the problems that current students are experiencing.

Creating these two versions of an academic vision helps the faculty honor the concept of high expectations by stretching both the faculty and the students. It also helps ensure that the expectations that are set by the academic mission are high but not unreasonable.

It simply doesn't make sense to tell teachers in a school where only 60 percent of the students are meeting state standards that next year they must ensure that 90 percent of the students will meet those standards. An academic mission that sets a target that is too high will likely result in a sense of hopelessness and even anger. Such a statement would most likely shift the dialogue to why 90 percent is an unrealistic target, a completely unproductive activity. It definitely does not motivate teachers to be proactive in their search for and use of more effective instructional practices that will help more students succeed. An expectation that is set too high creates a failure environment for both teachers and students. However, when the bar is set at a number that is 10 percent above the current level of student performance on state standards, teachers and students will see this as reasonable and attainable and will work to achieve or exceed that level. Such a goal will lead the teachers to the realization that they can help students succeed as learners. It also helps them understand that their journey toward the vision is made up of a series of small steps.

This commonsense approach is supported by research done by Wigfield, Eccles, and Rodriguez (1998). In their summary of findings regarding the nature of student motivation they reported, "When individuals think that they can accomplish a task, they are more likely to do so."

The academic mission is not a static target. Rather, it is a continuous improvement target. When the target expressed in the formative academic mission is consistently met, the faculty raises the bar and identifies a new and higher target. The raising of the bar is cause for school-wide celebration because the teachers, students, and principal have accomplished something of real significance! It is important to make it a major event.

Teachers have told us frequently that they find these two academic mission statements very helpful. The summative academic mission keeps the ultimate target in front of them. However it is the formative academic mission that helps them and their students stay motivated to keep improving. One teacher said, "It makes so much sense to break the ultimate target up into smaller, more doable targets. It helps me and most definitely helps my students." We refer to the formative academic mission as the engine that drives the Continuous Improvement System. It is the first document that the faculty writes.

Format and Process for Creating Both Versions of the Academic Mission

Formative Academic Mission Format

> We, the educators of _____School, ensure that _____ percent or more of our students will attain a minimum score of ____ percent correct responses on all formative assessments.

The formative academic mission statement clearly sets forth the desired level of academic achievement for a specified percentage of students. Using the provided format, faculty members decide what numbers will be used to fill in the blanks. When writing the formative academic mission, we recommend that they decide the second number first. This number sets the expected minimum level of achievement. Then the faculty must decide what percentage of students will be expected to reach that level.

When completed, this statement could read:

> We, the educators of _____ School, ensure that 80 percent or more of our students will attain a minimum score of 75 percent correct responses on all formative assessments.

We have found that it is very important to maintain the word "ensure" in both academic mission statements and the school vision statement because of the mindset that it creates. The word "ensure" is almost certain to be a topic of concern. People will say that they cannot ensure anything about student achievement and they will offer other words. One phrase that we frequently hear is "we will strive."

One way to clarify the power of the word "ensure" is to ask teachers to place their pens on the table in front of them and then ask them to "strive" to pick them up. After an awkward moment and few giggles, they realize that there is no "striving" to pick up the pencil. They either pick it up or they do not. Next ask teachers if they could ensure that 10 percent of their students will attain a minimum score of 10 percent correct on a test. The answer will be, "Yes." This short conversation demonstrates that the word "ensure" is not the issue. Rather, the numbers are the issue, and this is why the numbers must be realistic and attainable.

As with all documents in the CIS, it is critical that all faculty members actively participate in creating both the formative and summative academic mission statements.

Process for Creating the Formative Academic Mission

As we mentioned previously, the faculty writes this statement first as it drives both teacher and student performance throughout the school year.

1. The principal gathers the summative data for the past two years for specific grade levels or specific content areas. He schedules a work session and shares this data with faculty members, helping them analyze and discuss the data to get an accurate picture of how students in the school have performed in the past.
2. Faculty members engage in a dialogue designed to reach consensus on what currently constitutes the minimum acceptable level of formative academic performance in the school. This is usually considered to be a grade of 60 to 70 percent correct answers on a test. Teachers must bring their grade books to the work session and use them to calculate the percent of students who consistently achieve or exceed this grade in their individual classrooms.
3. The principal writes the format of the formative academic mission statement on a board or flip chart that is visible to the entire faculty. There are no numbers, only blank spaces followed by the percent signs.
4. The principal organizes the teachers in small groups and asks each group to come to consensus on the numbers to insert in the blank spaces. These numbers should slightly exceed the current level they identified in step 2. The intent is to move students and teachers just outside their comfort zone. If these numbers are reasonable and attainable, both teachers and students will rise to the challenge.
5. The principal asks one of the small groups to report its numbers. The numbers are recorded in two columns under the format statement. This continues with the other tables until all groups have posted their numbers.
6. The principal engages the groups in a dialogue about their reasons for selecting the numbers they chose.
7. Following the dialogue, the principal asks each group to again select the two numbers that they feel are most reasonable and attainable. Any group may change one or both of their numbers or keep them the same. Repeat the report and dialogue process described in steps 5 and 6 until consensus is reached.
8. The principal clarifies that this statement now applies to all classrooms and is nonnegotiable. All teachers must commit to helping their students reach

the performance level set in the academic mission. Minor adjustments may be allowed for honors classes. Also, this statement is not intended for special education classes where IEPs must be honored.

In the past, when the focus was exclusively on teaching, it was common practice for teachers to teach, test, and move to the next unit without fully understanding the achievement level of the individual student or the classroom as a whole. The formative academic mission changes that practice. It makes real-time student achievement data visible for all to see. It requires that the teacher reflect on the data, discuss it with colleagues, and then use the data to drive future instruction. It provides visible evidence of the impact individual teachers can have on student learning.

When the faculty writes the formative academic mission they are setting the standard for student performance during the school year. When this is done, the faculty turns their attention to writing the standard for student performance on the high-stakes test that occurs near the end of the school year. This is the summative academic mission.

Summative Academic Mission Format

We, the educators of _____ School, ensure that _____ percent or more of our students will attain a minimum level of "meets state standards" on the year-end state assessment.

When completed, the summative academic mission statement could read:

> We, the educators of _____ School, ensure that 70 percent or more of our students will attain a minimum level of "meets state standards" on the year-end state assessment.

The faculty can use the same process to write the summative academic mission that they used to write the formative academic mission. As with the development of the school vision, the writing process should not be rushed. It is important to take whatever time is necessary for people to feel comfortable with the levels that are set.

It is also important to remind everyone that the percentages are fluid and will change in the future. When students consistently attain the levels of achievement designated in these two statements, one or both of the numbers are raised to a new reasonable and attainable level. This raising of the bar is a cause for school-wide celebration. It signals a major achievement in students' academic performance and should be recognized by everyone associated with the school.

THE CORE COMMITMENTS

Statements that identify the values staff members hold in common are sometimes referred to as core values. We use a different term because we want to emphasize that some action must take place. We use the term core commitments to emphasize that people must make a commitment if they are going to act upon their values. Core commitments are not abstract concepts. For instance, someone might say that they value the opportunity to sit on the patio and read the morning paper. This statement does not carry with it a commitment to do this each morning. If it did, it would read, "I will sit on my patio for a minimum of a half hour each morning and read the paper."

Engaging a faculty in a dialogue about what they value is an important activity. Of greater importance is the commitment to exhibit the behaviors that embody the values and the commitment to hold self and others accountable for those behaviors.

The core commitments are statements that describe the behaviors all faculty members agree to exhibit in pursuit of the school vision and the academic mission. These statements are concise and measurable. They are not the type of philosophical statements you find in a school vision. Again, it is important to apply the principle of less is more. There should be no less than three and no more than five core commitment statements. The reason for the limited number is to create a sharp focus and to ensure that all faculty members know and understand the commitment they are making.

Unfortunately this part of the improvement process is often omitted. The faculty might think they could save some time by not developing the core commitments, but invariably this omission causes problems as the complexity of the work increases. Without these statements as a foundation for the collaborative relationship, a faculty may revert to previous ineffective behaviors or even choose to give up trying to improve their practice when the challenges seem overwhelming. Here is a core commitment statement example:

We, the faculty of _____ School, commit to:

- Work in collegial and collaborative instructional teams
- Use data to analyze student achievement and drive instruction
- Neither make nor accept excuses

Process for Creating the Core Commitments

1. The principal or a teacher who can comfortably command the attention of the full faculty should begin with a brief review of the academic mission. This will create a backdrop for the work that follows.
2. Place the faculty in small work groups and ask individual groups to list behaviors they feel are critical to accomplishing the academic mission.
3. Ask each group to share their statements and post the statements on a board that is visible to the entire faculty, omitting duplicates.
4. Because working in instructional teams is at the very heart of the CIS, we strongly suggest that "working in collegial and collaborative instructional teams" be a required core commitment. It is impossible to make system-level changes in instruction if educators do not work in collegial and collaborative instructional teams.
5. Ask the groups what they would see if the statements were put into action. Example: What would observers see if they sat in on a meeting of an instructional team?
6. Ask people to discuss the importance of their individual statements.
7. Ask each group to select four statements they deem most important. Groups may combine behaviors from two or more statements to more accurately reflect their opinions. However, we caution against the temptation to put too many behaviors into one statement.
8. Repeat the process until consensus is reached on three to five concise and measurable statements.

As with all the documents that are part of the CIS, it is important that you do not rush this process. Taking adequate time in the development process is of particular importance with the core commitments. Of the five documents, the core commitments are of the greatest importance in creating the desired culture. This is because the core commitments describe the essential behaviors that everyone must adopt to effectively collaborate as team members. As staff members learn to hold themselves and each other accountable for practicing these behaviors, the culture changes in a positive way.

THE MEETING NORMS

In a previous chapter we noted that most educators are not skilled in conducting a business meeting because they have not been trained to do so. This is true of both administrators and teachers. Unfortunately, this leads to meetings that are less than effective. Meetings are often held with no specific agenda and this results in valuable time wasted by social talk, war stories, and complaints. Typically, there is no clear process for identifying who is responsible to do what by when. As a result, little gets accomplished following the meeting and significant issues fall by the wayside. The good news is that meetings can be both productive and enjoyable. Even better news is that educators can easily learn the skills needed for an effective business meeting. They can plan and run their meetings (see chapter 4) so they provide a venue to get important tasks done, solve problems, celebrate success, and build camaraderie.

Meeting norms are an essential component of an effective meeting. The meeting norms should be limited to three to five statements that set the parameters for behavior during meetings. The people who will attend the meetings must write the norms. This ensures that they know and understand their commitment to follow the norms. Here is a meeting norms example:

We, the faculty of _____ School, commit to:

- Conduct each meeting according to an agenda
- Encourage the free flow of ideas
- Respect divergent opinions
- Carry out the decisions made in the meeting

The faculty can use the same procedures they used to create the shared vision, academic mission, and core commitments to write the norms. Once the norms are created, meeting facilitators must expect, encourage, and reinforce the need for all people to hold each other accountable to the norms during every meeting.

It has been our experience that the Pareto Principle (the "80/20 rule") comes into play with both the core commitments and the meeting norms. Eighty percent or more of the people tend to follow them and are open to feedback should they fail to do so. The remaining 20 percent of the people can hold the full faculty hostage by not following some or all of the core commitments or meeting norms. If this happens, it is essential for individuals to step up, identify the inappropriate behavior, and ask that the core commitments and meeting norms be honored.

A NORMS STORY

The full faculty had written the meeting norms and the core commitments. They even had a commitment ceremony. One staff member was absent the day the ceremony occurred. This same staff member had made several remarks about the "silliness of writing norms." "After all, we are all adults," he stated.

His colleagues were getting increasingly agitated because during staff meetings, he would interrupt when other people were talking and say things like, "That will never work with our kids." Or, "We tried that years ago and it didn't work." A few faculty members went to the principal and asked him to address this issue. The principal skillfully refused and coached them in ways they could hold the person accountable for the norm—"We honor all voices equally." Finally, during a meeting in which the offender cut people off four times, another teacher raised his hand and said, "Excuse me. I want to revisit one of our norms. It reads, 'We honor all voices equally. John, I am not sure if you are aware, but there is a pattern of behavior you display that is the opposite of this norm. When others are talking, you cut them off. And you also make excuses. I have noticed it several times during meetings and have not said anything. That is my fault. I should have asked you to observe our norm sooner. Thank you for listening to me."

Obviously, this intervention took considerable courage. For a few moments, everyone was silent. Then the offending teacher said, "Wow! No one has ever told me that I do that. Please, everyone, if I cut you off, let me know." He also thanked the teacher that provided the feedback. The principal thanked everyone for "breathing real life" into the meeting norms and went on with the agenda.

THE SCHOOL RULES

If any organization is to function in an effective and efficient manner, members of that organization must know and follow certain rules. In schools, it is typical for rules to vary from classroom to classroom. Students may be allowed to chew gum in one classroom and not in another. To not be considered as tardy by one teacher, students must be in their seats when the bell rings while simply being in the room is acceptable to another teacher. This lack of consistency with rules creates a chaotic environment for students—especially young students. It is important for a school to operate by a single set of well-known behavioral expectations. The number of rules should be limited to three to five statements. Fewer than three will not be comprehensive and more than five will be too difficult to remember. Here is a school rules example:

> We, the members of _____ School, commit to:
> - Demonstrate respect
> - Accept responsibility for our behaviour
> - Act in a safe and orderly manner

The term "member" in the example above represents administrators, faculty, staff, and students. The rules apply to everyone. If we as educators expect students to accept the responsibility to arrive to class on time, then the adults in the school must also be expected to arrive to work and to meetings on time. It is not acceptable for security personnel to discipline a student for wearing a cap in the building if they are also wearing one as part of a uniform.

The process for the creation of the prior documents can be used to create the school rules. If the rules of the school are well thought out, almost any behavioral expectation can be covered by a minimal number of statements. Demonstrating respect may be seen in adult-to-student interaction, student-to-student interaction, and the appropriate care of property. Accepting responsibility for behavior may be seen in the timely completion of work and by accepting consequences for inappropriate behavior without escalating the situation. Acting in a safe manner may mean not having a weapon on campus. When the rules are stated in general terms, teachers have the opportunity to teach the meaning of terms like respect, responsibility, and safe. For instance, teaching young students to raise their hand to be recognized is a specific behavior that fits under the general rule of demonstrating respect. Reminding adults to do the same during meetings also fits under this rule.

THE NEXT STEPS

When the key documents are completed, it is up to the principal to consistently engage the faculty in activities that take the printed documents from words and concepts to a reality in the day-to-day operation of the school. Here are some suggestions to accomplish this.

- Print the school vision, academic mission, and core commitments in a professional format and post them in every classroom and other prominent locations.
- Print the meeting norms on each meeting agenda.
- During a faculty meeting, ask small groups to discuss the meaning of the school vision and give examples of things they have done or observed that

demonstrate the school vision in action. Then have each group report to the entire faculty.

- During a faculty meeting, have teachers share the most current classroom academic mission data. In any given meeting, either the classroom data or the grade-level data (see chapter 10) can serve as the focus. Presenting and discussing this data allows the entire faculty to gain insight into the achievement level across the school. Grade-level teams or content department teams make note of areas of weaknesses that students demonstrate as they enter the next level and discuss ways of addressing the issue. These cross-grade-level and department observations and the resulting suggestions generate a rich dialogue concerning instructional strategies. As a result, teachers continue to add to their "teaching toolbox."
- Take every opportunity to highlight the core commitments, noting when and how they are and are not are being demonstrated.
- During a faculty meeting, ask individuals to share in small groups or with the entire faculty what they have done or observed that exemplify one or more of the core commitments.
- If one or more of the core commitments are not being demonstrated, engage the faculty in a frank discussion about this omission. At this point, the faculty must determine if the existing core commitment is to be honored or abandoned and replaced with a commitment that the faculty thinks is more important and they are willing to consistently demonstrate.
- Create and include a motto on all internal documents or displayed on banners. Students, as well as teachers, can be challenged to live up to the spirit of the motto.
- Discuss the school rules frequently with both students and faculty. Teachers should lead discussions on what the rules mean and how or if they are being followed. This may lead to a revision of the current language, the elimination of some rules, and the addition of new rules.
- Involve students in planning how to present the school rules to new students.

Throughout this chapter, we have repeatedly said that the creation of these documents requires time, effort, and thoughtful dialogue. We emphasize this one more time and guarantee that the result is well worth the effort. All of these documents are important individually, but when used collectively, they form the foundation of a truly professional and collaborative culture in the school.

Chapter Seven

A Different Look at Curriculum

WHAT TO TEACH AND WHEN TO TEACH IT

During recent years there has been a transition from a classroom that was under the complete control of the teacher to district-controlled curriculum and now to state-mandated curriculum.

Today, education is driven primarily by state-mandated curriculum standards and high-stakes tests. Under these current mandates, educators are faced with the challenge of preparing students to be successful on high-stakes tests despite concerns about the educational equity and quality of these tests.

Currently states mandate what is to be taught, districts determine when, but teachers still decide how. Therefore, it is important to encourage teachers to bring their individual ideas and creativity to the instructional process, as long as they teach the required content. The Continuous Improvement System provides a clear and effective process for doing this. The CIS makes it possible for teachers to vary the content sequence within a given academic quarter or semester as they work together to find the most effective and efficient ways to instruct their students. This is done in a collaborative environment where teachers develop and use an instructional calendar that ensures effective planning of what to teach and when to teach it.

THE PRE-HIGH-STAKES TEST CURRICULUM

In the majority of districts in the United States, the central office provides a detailed pacing guide or curriculum map that sets forth the scope and sequence for what to teach and when to teach it. While these documents are intended to assist teachers in planning their instruction, many teachers frequently ignore them because they feel the documents are not user friendly. Nevertheless, teachers feel considerable pressure to maintain the pace set forth in the document. Many teachers admit they actually do not understand how to use these documents and, as a result, revert to turning pages in the textbook and hoping that it covers all of the mandated standards.

The CIS approach is very different from the conditions described above. In this System, teachers carefully analyze the state's standards and the district's curriculum to identify the critical content. After identifying this critical content, they engage in a dialogue to determine the sequence of the instruction. They do this by dividing the critical content into three approximately equal sections to be taught over the first three-quarters of the school year. We designed the CIS this way because the state-administered high-stakes tests are typically conducted in the fourth quarter.

After "chunking" the content in this manner, teachers identify and sequence the most important objectives in the curriculum and begin creating their instructional calendars. We strongly encourage teachers to develop their instructional calendars one month at a time. This schedule provides an opportunity to adjust the pace of instruction so that it matches student progress. This is essential because, as every educator knows, students do not learn according to a written schedule. Instead, students learn at their own pace and are strongly influenced by their individual interests and abilities.

As teachers develop the instructional calendars, they schedule specific dates for administering formative assessments. These dates must be flexible, because in the CIS teachers monitor student progress on a daily basis to ensure that students are fully prepared before administering any assessment. An individual teacher or all the teachers on the team may discover that the pacing is too fast and that the students are not ready. It makes no sense to test on Thursday if the students are still struggling with Tuesday's content.

It is a common practice in many schools to administer an assessment on a regular schedule, perhaps every Friday. We do not recommend this practice, as it is too frequent and too rigid. It takes away valuable time that could be used for instruction and often interrupts the natural flow of a sequence of instruction. Instead, assessment should occur at the logical points in the unit of instruction and only when the teacher determines that the students are ready for the assessment.

We recommend that teachers of a grade level or content area create the common assessments (see chapter 9) as they develop their instructional calendars. This practice ensures a direct link among the content, the instruction, and the assessment. Fully understanding how a concept will be assessed assists the teacher in planning and choosing the instructional strategies to teach that concept.

The instructional calendar is a valuable planning tool in and of itself. However, the greatest benefit of this tool happens as a result of the dialogue that occurs among teachers as they create the calendar. This shared work provides the perfect opportunity for teachers to discuss the content, the sequence of instruction, and the method of assessment. It also gives them the time and opportunity to share instructional strategies with one another. This collaborative effort is critical to the development of a school culture focused on teaching and learning.

The principal plays a very important role in the collaborative instructional process. His role begins when he communicates the clear expectation that teachers work collaboratively in instructional teams as they develop the instructional calendars and the common assessments. He monitors the quality of the teachers' work by requiring the faculty to submit the instructional calendars and the common assessments on the first instructional day of each month. Holding individuals accountable to these expectations is an essential part of the principal's role. In addition, the principal must provide the support and professional development the teachers need in order to meet the expectations. This theme of high demand and high support is consistent throughout the CIS.

Teachers generally find it takes a little more time to develop the instructional calendars during the first year. However, as they become more skilled and comfortable in the process, the amount of time they spend in this activity decreases. As teachers follow the instructional calendar they record any adjustments required for a given unit. Each year of planning provides insight into the next year's planning. These notes are of significant value when they develop the instructional calendars during the following year as they help teachers continuously improve the scope and sequence of their instructional calendars.

State academic standards are typically identified by a codification system. One example of such a system breaks the academic standards down by Strand, Concept, and Performance Objective. For example, Strand 1 is Number Sense, Concept 2 within this strand is Numerical Operations, and Performance Objective 6 within this concept is division by a one-digit divisor. The codes may be abbreviated as S1-C2-PO6 or more simply 1-2-06. These codes will vary from state to state. Table 7.1 is an example of an instructional calendar.

Following is a two-week calendar example.

Table 7.1.   Example of an Instructional Calendar

Teacher	Grade level /Content Area			Month
Monday	*Tuesday*	*Wednesday*	*Thursday*	*Friday*
New Content S1-C2-PO6 Division with a single-digit divisor	*New Content* S1-C2-PO6 Division with a single-digit divisor	*New Content* S1-C2-PO6 Division with a single-digit divisor *Review Content* S1-C2-PO5 Multiply two-digit numbers by two-digit numbers	*New Content* S1-C2-PO6 Division with a single-digit divisor	*New Content* S1-C2-PO6 Division with a single-digit divisor
New Content S3-C3-PO 1, 2 & 3 Solve one-step equations with a single variable *Review Content* S1-C2-PO13 Order of operations	*New Content* S3-C3-PO 1, 2 & 3 Solve one-step equations with a single variable	*New Content* S3-C3-PO 1, 2 & 3 Solve one-step equations with a single variable	*New Content* S3-C3-PO 1, 2 & 3 Solve one-step equations with a single variable	Formative Assessment #1 (Division & Equations)

As you examine this two-week calender please keep in mind:

1. There is no reference to a textbook chapter or page number on the calendar.
2. The content is identified by the state standards code and a brief description. The inclusion of the code ensures that teachers are focused on the state standards and not simply turning pages in the textbook. The description makes it easy for students to understand what they are to learn.
3. Teachers are required to post the objective for each lesson at the front of the classroom. The teachers must adjust the language of the objective to the learning level of the students and present the objective in "student-friendly" language. To create an effective introduction to the instruction, teachers must talk to the students about the objective in a way that ensures that students know what they are doing and why they are doing it.
4. Both new and review objectives are included on the instructional calendar. The review objectives are an important aspect of successful instruction. The review spirals high-priority objectives throughout the year to ensure retention. Review objectives can also be used with a recent topic that proved to be difficult for students. This is not intended to be a full lesson

and can be taught as a transitional activity. For instance, the teacher might write a problem associated with the review content on the board as students return from lunch and ask them to work in pairs to solve the problem. Such an activity would focus the students on math and give the teacher an indication of the students' knowledge of the review performance objective.

5. The formative assessments are numbered, described, and included in the instructional calendar. This makes identifying the assessment easier on the data charts described in chapter 10.
6. The instructional calendar is posted in the classroom next to the academic mission, the core commitments, and the school rules.

Item 2 in the preceding list is of particular importance. As we mentioned at the start of this chapter, it has been common practice for the textbook to serve as the curriculum. Teachers would open the book to page 1 on the first day of school and continue turning the pages until the final day of school. This practice is totally unacceptable in today's educational environment. Because today's curriculum is dictated by state standards, the textbook must now be viewed as one of many tools used to teach the required standards. Simply teaching one page after another will only guarantee that time will be wasted teaching content that is not required. It also opens the door to missing standards not covered in the textbook or not getting to required objectives that appear so close to the end of the book that they would be taught after the high-stakes test is administered.

We suggest educators use a proper amount of skepticism as they consider claims by textbook companies that their book directly correlates to state standards. The safest and most professional way of using a textbook is to take each state standard and locate where that content is presented in the book. Teachers should record the location of the content standards for easy reference when creating the instructional calendars. Because some standards will not be found in the book, this process of matching the standards to the text will alert teachers to the fact that they must find alternative materials for some of the mandated curriculum.

THE POST-HIGH-STAKES TEST CURRICULUM

As a rule, there are several weeks remaining in the school year following the high-stakes test. This is valuable time and we suggest that the faculty devote it to preparing students to succeed in the next grade level or subject.

Immediately following the high-stakes test, the principal should schedule cross-grade-level or common-subject meetings. For example, fourth-grade teachers should identify for third-grade teachers the skills that are essential for success in the fourth grade. Fourth-grade teachers also should note any pattern of weak skills with which previous students have entered the grade. Third-grade teachers must then devote their undivided attention to ensuring that students master those skills and enter the fourth grade fully prepared to succeed. It is important for the principal to prepare the faculty for these meetings. He does this by defining the purpose and clearly stating that this is a collaborative activity and not a finger-pointing activity. The goal is enhanced student performance and these meetings must not be allowed to deteriorate into blame sessions.

In the elementary school another way of making optimal use of this time is to physically assign students to their teacher for the next year after the high-stakes test is complete. This enables the teacher to get to know the new students and develop a classroom culture. The new teacher can now assess the skills of the incoming students and personally prepare them for success at the next level.

As a result of using the System, teachers become skilled in working together to solve problems. The grade-level to grade-level or content-area to content-area exchange described is intended to be collaborative and non-threatening. Teachers become so committed to ensuring that all students learn that they want to know what and how they can improve so that students succeed as they transition to the next level.

SAM'S STORY

Sam is a highly experienced fifth-grade teacher. During the first year that his school was implementing the system, he was often heard to say, "I have been doing this for a long time; just leave me alone to teach my kids." He sat alone during faculty meetings and rarely contributed during Instructional Team meetings. He steadfastly refused to participate in creating the instructional calendar. His grade-level colleagues were very frustrated by his behavior and began to ignore him, and this was just what he wanted.

He did, however, maintain the classroom data chart that was required by the principal. Near the end of the first semester, the principal met with Sam and began the meeting by placing Sam's classroom chart on the desk along with the charts from the other three teachers in the fifth grade. The principal asked Sam to describe what he saw. Sam had to admit that the scores in his classroom were significantly lower than in the other classrooms.

The principal did not dwell on this and instead asked Sam to identify his concerns with the Continuous Improvement System. Sam's response was a general, "I just like what I do better." The principal replied, "This is not about you; it is about what your students are, or more importantly, are not learning. So let's see if we can identify the specific issues that keep you from collaborating with your colleagues."

The principal then walked Sam through every component of the CIS, beginning with the school vision statement. After explaining each component, the principal asked Sam what his specific concern was. Sam had difficulty in identifying specific concerns with any of the individual components. When he did express a specific concern the principal was able to help him work through it. In the end, Sam had no arguments left.

The principal began to attend all fifth-grade Instructional Team meetings and focused on drawing Sam into the dialogue and highlighting any positive ideas Sam offered. As time passed, Sam became more comfortable with the team process and his colleagues learned that he had valuable contributions to offer. As a result of the collaborative effort, the scores in Sam's classroom began to climb.

During the final faculty meeting of the year, Sam asked to speak. He offered an apology to his colleagues and to his students. He said, "I was wrong; you can teach an old dog new tricks."

Chapter Eight

Instruction

THE FOUNDATION OF EFFECTIVE TEACHING

The job of the educator is to inspire, to encourage, and to empower. He does this by consistently providing high-quality instruction that helps students master critical content and apply this knowledge in real-life situations. This is one of the most difficult jobs in the world. It is also one of the most gratifying.

Numerous studies have addressed the impact of effective instruction on student achievement. A McREL policy brief (Miller 2003) reported on a 1994 study conducted by Sanders and Horn that revealed a 39 percentage point difference in student achievement between classrooms headed by "most effective" teachers and those taught by "least effective" teachers. In classrooms under the direction of "most effective" teachers, students posted an average gain of 53 percentage points over one academic year. In classrooms under the direction of "least effective" teachers, the average gain was only 14 percentage points.

In this chapter, we provide a variety of suggestions for what teachers and instructional leaders can do to continuously improve instructional practices through the implementation of the Continuous Improvement System.

WHAT DO YOU NEED FOR EFFECTIVE INSTRUCTION?

A Constantly Expanding Collection of Instructional Strategies

Two well-known researchers, Bruce Joyce and Beverly Showers, published the results of a 1980 study that demonstrated a very important fact about teaching. In *Student Achievement through Staff Development* (1988), they wrote that the more instructional strategies a teacher used, the higher the level of academic achievement by the students. That is a very powerful statement. It certainly makes a case for all teachers developing a substantial repertoire of instructional strategies. This statement by Joyce and Showers fueled a flurry of staff development for teachers all over the United States. Teachers learned about learning styles and associated strategies. They learned about using cooperative learning strategies to help students work in groups. They learned about thinking skills to help implement Benjamin Bloom's taxonomy. These are but a few of the well-attended and well-intended staff development efforts from the 1980s and the 1990s.

Unfortunately, these staff development endeavors produced very little change in the practice of most teachers. This happened because the majority of teachers did one of two things. One, they attended the session as a compliant participant. They then returned to the classroom and reverted back to their well-ingrained and comfortable practices which were typically small in number. Two, they attended the session with enthusiasm and returned to the classroom eager to try the new strategy. They tried it with their students a time or two and if it did not produce immediately visible results, they discarded the strategy and then went back to only using their well-ingrained and comfortable practices. For most teachers this was simply teaching by telling. Lecture was, and still is, the predominant method of instruction. This is not to say that it is a bad strategy. Used with skill and with moderation, it is very effective, especially with students who tend to learn in a more auditory way.

The failure to successfully implement new strategies learned in the workshops was exacerbated by the fact that when teachers returned to their classrooms they continued to work as private practitioners. There was little or no opportunity to talk with colleagues about the new strategies they had just learned or to plan together about how and when to best use them. Teachers that did use the strategy had no chance to discuss how well it worked or to problem solve if it failed. Most importantly, assessment of students' success was typically not done until the end of a complete unit of instruction. Consequently, the teacher could not determine whether a particular strategy had helped students learn a specific curriculum item.

We do not intend this to be a "how to teach" chapter. Rather, it is a chapter that explains "how to collaborate to improve instructional practice." We want to help educators find, develop and use a continuously expanding collection of instructional strategies that they know work for them and their students because the student performance data demonstrates that they are effective.

We view high-quality teaching as one of the most difficult jobs in the world to do well consistently. It is a very complex activity that is heavily dependent upon the quality of the interaction between the teacher and the student. Each teacher brings his own individual strengths to the classroom. Given this, it is inappropriate for anyone to suggest that there is a "best way" to teach. In order to be truly successful, we believe that each teacher must acquire a repertoire of strategies and then make intelligent decisions about the use of any given strategy in the context of any given lesson.

Dr. Madeline Hunter often described teaching as having both an artistic facet and a scientific facet. The scientific facet is seen in the breadth and depth of the teacher's knowledge of proven instructional skills. The artistic facet is seen in the quality of the teacher's decisions as to how and when to apply specific instructional skills.

In conversations with Dr. Skoglund, she clearly stated that the intent of her work was to encourage teachers to make conscious and informed decisions as they planned and delivered their instruction. She did not intend the instructional skills that she identified to be used by teachers as a lock-step approach to instruction nor by administrators as an evaluation tool. Ultimately, what she accomplished was to create a common language for educators to use in dialogues about instruction.

When teachers meet in their instructional teams to establish the instructional calendar, they have the opportunity to talk about strategies they might use to teach upcoming lessons. The objective of this dialogue is to apply Joyce and Shower's wisdom and ensure the use of varied instructional strategies. Teachers can do this by:

- Sharing the strategies they already know and starting a glossary of these strategies that they can teach to one another.
- Attending professional development sessions together with the intent of adding to their collection of instructional strategies.
- Studying professional literature. Two excellent resources for such an activity are *Designing and Teaching Learning Goals and Objectives* (2002) and *What Works in Schools* (2003), by Robert Marzano.
- Using as a resource and a guide an instructional coach who provides feedback that helps the teacher learn to use new strategies effectively.
- Observing a colleague teaching a lesson and naming the strategies observed. This is helpful because often teachers use an effective strategy at an unconscious level. They don't even realize they are using it because it comes so naturally for them. When a colleague observes a strategy in action, and names that strategy, it is helpful for the teacher being observed for two reasons. First, it takes the skill from the unconscious to the conscious level and consequently its use becomes more intentional. Second, it can be added to the collection of instructional strategies of all teachers once it is identified.

Generating a shared collection of strategies is the starting point. However, the ultimate goal is to increase teachers' successful use of these varied strategies. To do this, teachers should dedicate some of their collaboration time to discussing the effectiveness level of the instruction. As the trust level grows, the teachers can be very honest with one another when a strategy just did not work. There are several things colleagues can do to help a teacher who had trouble with a strategy. These include:

• Determine if it was the right strategy for the content.
• Determine if it was the right time to use that strategy in light of where students were in learning that content.
• Determine if the strategy was used correctly.
• Determine what the teacher could have done differently.

The next several pages are devoted to an overview of Madeline Hunter's work. For educators who have been teaching for several years this may seem redundant because they previously learned about her work and have been using it. However, with our penchant in education for the newest, greatest, and latest thing, we often discard older collections of solid wisdom. Her work is one of those things that has been labeled as "dated." If dated means it is something that was written more than five years ago, yes—her work is dated. If dated means no longer valid, this term does not apply. It is for that reason we include this review/introduction of her wisdom. We think her work, one of the "tried-and-true" developments in education, is worth a new or a second look. Whether it is a new or a second look will depend on the reader's years in the teaching profession.

In her book, *Mastery Teaching*, (1982) Dr. Hunter identified four Essential Elements of Instruction:

1. Select an objective at the correct level of difficulty for the students.
2. Teach to the objective.
3. Monitor the learning and adjust the instruction.
4. Apply the principles of learning.

We have included her wisdom because these skills are common sense and germane to effective instruction at all grade levels and content areas. They ensure that the teacher fully understands what the students are expected to learn in a given lesson. They help the teacher generate interest in the topic and engage students in situations that will help them recall the content of the lesson. They help the teacher eliminate extraneous information and activities and carefully focus the instruction on the identified objective. They help the teacher monitor student understanding frequently and adjust the instruction according to student needs.

Dr. Hunter's Essential Elements of Instruction are compatible with the instructional strategies that are a part of Cooperative Learning, Mastery Learning, Inquiry Learning, Learning Styles, Thinking Skills, and Effective Lecture. Because we consider the "tried-and-true" wisdom of Madeline Hunter a foundation to good instruction, we offer this review/introduction of her work. Text box 8.1 provides a brief overview of the Essential Elements of Instruction. The text boxes that follow explain the what, when, why, and how of each element. The numbers that appear do not suggest a sequence of instruction; they are included only to assist the reader in making the connection between the initial overview and the information that follows. Note all the examples cited in the text boxes 8.1 through 8.11 refer to the example lesson and problems shown on page 81.

Overview of Hunter's Essential Elements of Instruction

1. Instructional Objective	2. Task Analysis
• Identify the specific content / skill • Identify the level of thinking required • Identify the specific desired student performance	• Identify the outcome objective • Identify critical sub-objectives • Sequence the critical sub-objectives
3. Teach to the Objective	4. Monitor Student Performance and Adjust the Instruction
• Teach one sub-objective at a time • Match information to the sub-objective • Match questions to the sub-objective • Match activities to the sub-objective • Match feedback on student performance to the sub-objective	• Teach one sub-objective at a time • Match information to the sub-objective • Match questions to the sub-objective • Match activities to the sub-objective • Match feedback on student performance to the sub-objective

5. Principles of learning

A. Anticipatory Set
   • Generate overt/covert behavior from all students
   • Call attention to past experiences
   • Show connection between past experience and present learning

B. Active Participation
   • Generate overt/covert behavior from all students
   • Consistently engage all students in the learning activity

C. Motivation to Learn
   • Level of concern (raise/lower)
   • Knowledge of results (specific/immediate)
   • Success (individual/group)
   • Interest (vivid/importance)
   • Feeling Tone (impact of pleasant vs. unpleasant)

D. Assessment
   • Match content to final objective
   • Match format to high-stakes test

F. Closure
   • Generate overt/covert behavior
   • Match activity to sub-objectives and final objective

E. Retention
   • Meaning (create understanding of why learning is important)
   • Modeling (demonstrate/label a perfect performance)
   • Practice (monitor performance on sub-objectives and final objective)

Textbox 8.1 Overview of Hunters Essential Elements of Instruction

1. *INSTRUCTIONAL OBJECT*

What:

This is a written statement that defines <u>exactly</u> what the student is to learn and how the student will demonstrate that the knowledge / skill has been acquired.

When:

- Long term – identify the final outcome of a unit of instruction
- Short term – identify the specific objective or sub-objectives of the lesson

Why:

- Clarity – when this is clear it makes it easier for the teacher to plan and the student to understand what he is to learn
- Focus – when the objective is clearly communicated to students, they are better prepared to receive the instruction
- Monitoring – when the desired outcome is clear, formative and summative assessments are easier to create and more accurately measure student progress

How:

A well thought out instructional objective should address three areas:

1. The objective must clearly identify the level of performance required. The use of Bloom's taxonomy will assist both the teacher and the student to focus on the learning.
2. The objective must clearly identify the content or desired outcome of the lesson.
3. The objective must clearly identify how the student will be expected to demonstrate understanding of the content that has been presented.

It is important to post the objective – in student-friendly language – in the classroom to ensure students know what it is that they are doing.

Example: The learner will correctly apply the factor tree method by using the process to find the lowest common denominator of two common fractions.

Textbox 8.2 Instructive Objective

2. *TASK ANALYSIS*

What:

This is the teacher's ability to break the instructional objective into critical and logical subobjectives.

Why:

- Clarity — when it is clear in the teacher's mind, the content of the lesson is easier to plan
- Focus — students will find it easier to follow instruction that is logical and sequential
- Monitoring — this makes it possible for the teacher to identify and correct specific student errors

When:

- Long term — prior to any significant unit of instruction
- Short term — prior to any given lesson
- Immediate — during the lesson if students are experiencing difficulty

How:

Learning is a complex activity and teachers must clearly understand what the student is to do and how to do it if the instruction is to be efficient and effective. Work through the following:

1. Clarify the objective — know exactly what the student is being asked to do
2. Identify critical vocabulary
3. Identify and sequence critical subobjectives
4. Consider the inclusion of noncritical content if it will enhance meaning and interest

Example: Prior to finding the lowest common denominator using the factor tree, the student must understand the definitions of denominator and factor.

Textbox 8.3 Task Analysis

3. *TEACHING TO THE OBJECTIVE*

What:

This is the teacher's ability to focus the instruction on one clear objective at a time. It includes both teacher and student activities.

When:

- Whenever direct instruction is taking place
- When new or complicated material is presented
- When students are experiencing difficulty

Why:

For the teacher
- It saves time
- It helps students stay on task
- Students learn more and require less reteaching
- It makes monitoring easier

For the student
- It helps to maintain focus
- It makes learning easier and faster
- It allows better retention
- Success leads to a desire to continue the learning

How:

High-quality instruction is sequential and easy for the student to follow. It is void of superfluous information and activities. When planning a lesson, a teacher should:

- Teach the subobjectives in sequence and focus on only one at a time
- Keep all information and demonstrations directly focused on the instructional objective
- Keep all questions (both teacher and student) directly focused on the instructional objective
- Ensure that all guided practice activities are directly focused on the instructional objective
- Provide feedback to students that is directly focused on the instructional objective
- At the end of the lesson, put the pieces together and show students how the form a whole

  Example: In teaching students to use the factor tree to find the lowest common denominator, ensure an understanding of the vocabulary and how to identify prime factors before demonstrating how to do the entire process.

Textbox 8.4 Teaching the Objective

4. *MONITOR AND ADJUST*

What:

This is the teacher's ability to check on the learning of each student during the instruction and make changes to the instructional strategies if students are experiencing difficulty.

Why:

- Student errors must be identified and corrected before incorrect learning becomes ingrained.
- Early correction of errors saves time in the reteaching process.
- This allows students to correct errors early and experience more success
- Higher levels of student achievement reduce discipline issues

When:

- Student performance should be monitored after each sub-objective, during guided practice and closure.
- Instructional strategies should be adjusted when students already know the content or when they are experiencing difficulty.

How:

A teacher must be constantly aware of how well students are grasping the material in the lesson. Checking on student progress only at the end of the lesson or by looking at last night's homework is too late. As a lesson proceeds, the teacher must keep in mind:

- You can not see what is in a student's mind and so it is imperative that overt behavior is frequently generated.
- Look and listen carefully. Be aware of any frustration that becomes apparent and adjust the level of difficulty.
- Seize the teachable moment. Don't just hope that the light will go on.
- If the lesson is a disaster, stop and come back tomorrow with a better plan.

    Example: As I have walked around the room, I am aware that several of you are struggling with the final step. Students, please watch carefully as I demonstrate that again and then I will ask you to work a problem with a partner to ensure that everyone understands.

Textbox 8.5 Monitor and Adjust

5A. *ANTICIPATORY SET*

What:

This is the teacher's ability to bring forth in the students' minds past knowledge or experiences that relate directly to what the students are about to learn.

Why:

- It grabs the students' attention
- It creates a link to past learning
- It signals that new learning is about to begin
- It creates enthusiasm for what is to be learned

When:

- Prior to the start of instruction
- Between major sub-objectives
- After an interruption to the instruction

How:

The teacher must plan an activity that piques the students' curiosity about what they are going to learn and connects it to something they know.

- Engage the students either overt (tell, write, draw) or covert (recall, imagine, think about) activity
- Connect the past learning to the new learning. There is no need to dwell on this. This is a brief activity intended to prepare students to learn something new. It may be as simple as recalling how yesterday's lesson ended and how that has prepared students to proceed today.
- Give a rationale as to why the new learning is important
- Be specific! Do not lead the students astray with a vague anticipatory set. If none comes to mind, just begin the instruction.

  Example: Recall your first experience with finding the lowest common denominator. How did you go about doing this?

Textbox 8.6 Anticipatory Set

5B. *ACTIVE PAARTICIPATION*

What:	Why:

What:

This is the teacher's ability to maintain the students' mental involvement in the learning.

When:

- All the time!
- This is especially important during the anticipatory set, teacher demonstration, guided practice and during closure.

Why:

For the teacher
- The teacher learns who knows what
- Accurate monitoring of student progress can not be done without this
- It allows the teacher to make appropriate adjustments in instruction
- It maintains student focus and reduces discipline problems

For the student
- It helps the student maintain focus
- Students remember what they do
- It generates greater student interest

How:

Just listening and watching does not allow optimal learning for most students. Students learn faster and remember longer when they are actively involved in the learning.

- Generate covert behavior in students by using words like: visualize, think about, prepare to explain and imagine.
- Generate overt behavior in students by using words like: write, solve, explain to a partner and demonstrate at the board.
- Engage all the students. Do not let students hide by calling on only students who raise their hands or ones that you believe will know the correct answer. Ask the question, allow think time and then call on someone to answer.

Example: Think about the factor tree process that we have just learned. Solve the problem that I have on the board and be prepared to explain to the class how you did it.

Textbox 8.7 Active Participation

5C. *MOTIVATION*

What:

This is the teacher's ability to trigger the students' intent or desire to learn.

Why:

- This focuses the students' attention.
- It generates higher levels of student success.
- It increases students' willingness to try.

When:

- All the time!
- Especially when a critical point in the lesson is reached or if students' attention is wandering.

How:

Remember that motivation is a personal and internal drive. It can not be injected into a student. Create the conditions under which students will choose to become involved.

- Raise the level of concern. Use questioning strategies that make each student anticipate that they may be the one called on to respond.
- Provide immediate and very specific feedback. When students know the result of their effort, they are better able to self correct and experience success.
- Build in success. This is the single most powerful experience that drives students to continue learning. Monitor effectively to ensure that everyone is prepared prior to an assignment or test.
- Maintain interest in the content by infusing novelty or demonstrating the importance of the content.
- Keep the feeling tone in the room appropriate. Students are willing to risk in an environment that they feel is safe and will withdraw if the environment is threatening.

    Example: Congratulations! Everyone did the last problem correctly. Now I know that you are prepared to go on to the next step in the process.

Textbox 8.8 Motivation

5D. *ASSESSMENT*

What:

This is the teacher's ability to accurately determine who has learned what. This may be done following instruction on critical sub-objectives, following instruction on a terminal objective or at the end of a complete unit of instruction. This may or may not be a graded activity.

When:

- Following any closure activity.
- Whenever it is appropriate to monitor students' progress.

Why:

- For the teacher:
1. This allows the teacher to monitor student progress and adjust the instruction in order to correct errors.
2. This keeps students actively involved in the learning process.

- For the student:
1. This provides an opportunity for the student to self-check and correct learning.
2. This promotes retention.
3. This creates a focus on the learning and not the activity.

How:

This activity clarifies, for both the student and the teacher, whether or not students have understood the instruction and are able to effectively use what they have learned.

- Match the content of the assessment directly to the learning objective.
- Include an optimal number of assessment items to accurately determine what students have learned.
- Match the content, language, and the format of the assessment directly to the high-stakes test.

    Example: Use the factor tree method to find the lowest common denominator for the following sets of common fractions. You are expected to show your work.

Textbox 8.9 Assessment

5E. *RETENTION*

What:

This is the teacher's ability to involve students in an experience that they will remember and be able to apply to future learning.

Why:

- This promotes student success in both current and future learning
- This creates a link to future learning
- Less review/reteach activities are required
- This allows more content to be introduced and mastered

When:

- All the time!
- Especially when critical subobjectives or terminal objectives are taught
- When closure is brought to a critical component of the lesson

How:

The student will not benefit from learning something that cannot later be recalled and applied. Remember to spiral learning throughout the year, something that is experienced once will not be committed to long-term memory.

- Enhance understanding by demonstrating the value of the content, use vivid charts and organizers, involve multiple learning modes, and link the learning to something that is important in the students' life.
- Model a perfect performance and label the components that make the performance correct.
- Repeatedly practice correct performances.
- Keep the environment positive as students naturally protect themselves from unpleasant situations.

  Example: Notice in my example that I am circling the prime factors in red. If you will circle the prime factors, it will help you to quickly identify them as you prepare for the last step in the process.

Textbox 8.10 Retention

5F. *CLOSURE*

What:

This is the teacher's ability to engage the students in a process that will summarize and engrain the learning that they have just experienced.

When:

- Following any significant sub-objective or terminal objective.
- At the end of a lesson.
- Just before dismissal of the class.

Why:

For the teacher:
- To monitor who has learned what.
- This provides a starting point for the next segment of instruction.
- This maintains student involvement.

For the student:
- This is a self-check point.
- This promotes retention.
- This creates a focus on the learning and not the activity.
- This allows an opportunity for students to learn from each other.

How:

This is an activity that pulls everything together for the students. It is a final chance for the teacher to monitor student progress and correct errors before students are asked to work independently.

- This is a student activity — not a teacher activity.
- It is critical that overt activity is generated. Students must not only process the learning mentally; they must demonstrate their understanding in an observable manner.
- The activity must be directly related to the critical subobjective or the terminal objective of the lesson.

    Example: Please write something in your notes that will help you to remember this process. In a moment, I will ask a couple of you to share what you have written.

Textbox 8.11 Closure

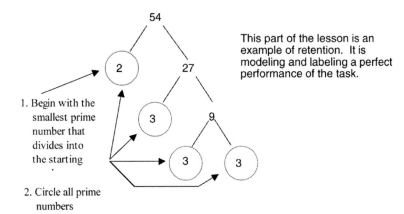

This part of the lesson is an example of retention. It is modeling and labeling a perfect performance of the task.

1. Begin with the smallest prime number that divides into the starting

2. Circle all prime numbers

Practice

135

Find the prime factors

This part of the lesson is an example of retention because it has students practice a correct performance.

A / 60   B / 28

Find the prime factors of two denominators

X / 24   Y / 30

Find the common denominator by finding the product of each prime factor taken the greatest number of times that it occurs in either denominator

Exit Problem

Find the LCD for:

3 / 32 and 11 / 90   A 270   B 720   **C 1440**   D 2880

This part of the lesson is an example of closure. Students are asked to demonstrate their understanding.

Figure 8.1

Again, we stress that this information is not a directive as to *the* way to teach. It is offered as a way to generate dialogue among teachers and to encourage them to explore a variety of instructional strategies that may benefit their students. Because our many years of educational experience has led us to believe that there is no one way to teach, there is no one way to coach a teacher to better instruction. It is our firm belief that improved instruction is best achieved through dialogue with individual teachers, and we spend considerable time having these dialogues with teachers.

Our experience has convinced us that one-on-one coaching interaction with teachers is the optimal way to ensure that teachers actually use new strategies, use them correctly, and make them a permanent part of their repertoire of strategies. When teachers have a rich collection of strategies from which to choose they are able to plan more effective lessons, teach more effectively, and adjust when in the middle of a lesson things are not going as well as they could. We think that because it is very difficult for the individual teacher to develop this collection, the collaborative element of the Continuous Improvement System makes it much more likely that teachers can improve their own practice and help colleagues do the same. The CIS helps create the culture necessary for the continuous professional growth of individual teachers and teams of teachers at grade levels and across content areas.

At various places in this book you have read about our intent to include some of the tried-and-true research and proven practice wisdom that exists in our profession. We have just shared a review of the work of Madeline Hunter as one example of that wisdom. Additional instructional strategies are provided in the appendix so that teachers will have the opportunity to consider and discuss strategies that are most appropriate for them to use.

Another powerful example is that of Benjamin Bloom's Taxonomy of Cognitive Skills. In this work he differentiated different kinds of thinking for different purposes. He also categorized the "thinking" verbs in our English language to make it possible for educators to more effectively facilitate and coach the thinking of their students. A third critical part of his work was the various assessment formats he suggested so that a teacher can more effectively determine if the thinking process of the student was producing the desired result. The Textbox 8.12 provides some detailed information about Bloom's Taxonomy. This is a powerful teaching tool that has been available to teachers for decades. Unfortunately, like so many worthy ideas, it was a commonly used tool for a period of time and then was pushed from the teacher's toolbox by the next new innovation.

Level	Verb Used	Assessment Format
Remembering: The student can recall or remember information in the same form that it was learned	Duplicate, identify, label, list, locate, match, memorize,name, recall, recognize, repeat, reproduce, select	Crossword puzzle, flash cards, individual recitation, pencil and paper test, thumbs up/down

Remembering is embedded in each advancing level.

Level	Verb Used	Assessment Format
Understanding: The student can explain or interpret information based on prior learning.	Define in own words, demonstrate, describe, explain, give example, interpret, praphrase, restate, review, rewrite, summarize	Biographical sketch, essay, glossary, interview, journal, oral response, panel discussion, role play, summary

Level	Verb Used	Assessment Format
Applying: The student can use prior learning to solve a new problem with little direction.	Apply, assemble, compute, demonstrate, diagram, employ, exhibit, perform, show, simulate, solve	Complete a process, conduct a lab experiment, construct a model, follow steps in a process, report and apply research

Level	Verb Used	Assessment Format
Analyzing: The student can examine and distinguish betweem data and draw conclusions.	Analyze, compare, contrast, criticize, diagram, distinguish between, examine, organize, probe, relate, separate	Analyze data, chart, display, essay flow chart, graph, map, PowerPoint presentation, timeline, write article

Level	Verb Used	Assessment Format
Evaluating: The student can make and justify a decision.	Argue, appraise, criticize, debate, defend, justify, rate, recommend, value	Editorial, debate in a book review, movie review or trial setting, plan an election campaign, write a consumer report

Level	Verb Used	Assessment Format
Creating: The student can combine facts and ideas to create a new product.	Assemble, combine, compose, construct, create, develop, formulate, imagine, invent	Debate, essay, create a game, photo essay, write a poem, play, song, or story, video

Textbox 8.12 Bloom's Taxonomy of Cognitive Skills

WHAT YOU DO NOT NEED FOR EFFECTIVE INSTRUCTION

This "do not need" information may be surprising as it eliminates a long-standing tradition in the teaching profession. Our do not need suggestion applies to a lesson plan. A lesson plan is a paper document that reads like a script of the lesson. The detail in the plan depends on the requirements set by either the school or the district.

There are many reasons teachers do not like the process of developing a lesson plan:

1. Writing this plan takes a considerable amount of time. Since many teachers teach more than one content area, this is a significant reason many teachers do not like planning lessons.
2. Because teachers write these plans in isolation, they can easily fall into the trap of compliance. They write the lesson plan to get it done, not to ensure that students learn what they are supposed to learn.
3. They write the lesson plan, they turn it in, and the principal puts a check mark behind the name of the teacher. This adds to the compliance pattern of writing the plan to "get it done" versus the "commitment to make the planning positively impact student learning."
4. Because they do have the big picture in mind, that is, where this lesson fits with the high-stakes tests, they tend to (a) repeat what they have done in the past with this content even when the data indicates that the students were not successful on this particular element on the high-stakes test and (b) plan a series of activities that keep the students busy rather than provide a focused objective that gives the student a target for learning.

It does not apply to lesson planning. Lesson planning is a critical activity that teachers collaboratively accomplish based on their knowledge of the state- and district-mandated curriculum. Because they know what will be tested, they know what they should teach to help their students score high on these tests.

To understand the value of "lesson planning" over "lesson plans" it is important to consider some things about lesson planning.

In contrast to creating a paper document, lesson planning provides the teacher with an opportunity to work in a collaborative environment where the focus is joint planning of curriculum and dialogue about instructional strategies. This collaborative lesson planning is an essential element of the Continuous Improvement System. During the lesson planning process, teachers meet in instructional teams and engage in a dialogue to:

- Plan and produce the instructional calendar

- Plan and produce common assessments
- Plan how and when to administer those assessments in order to produce real-time student achievement data
- Disaggregate data and complete error analysis of student work
- Analyze data, share successful instructional strategies, and develop new instructional strategies
- Plan the reteach/retest process
- Evaluate student achievement across the school and engage in professional development designed to improve instructional practices

The process sets in motion a positive-impact spiral. The more teachers collaboratively plan, the better the students perform. The better the students perform, the more committed the teachers become to collaborative lesson planning. The result is that they will accomplish everything a paper lesson plan produces and more. The important "more" is greater collaboration, significantly higher levels of student achievement, and the data to show it.

Initially, lesson planning may take slightly more time than the development of a traditional lesson plan. However, as teachers become more skilled in lesson planning, they will become more efficient with the process.

The additional staff time made available to teachers to engage in collegial activities designed to change their instructional practices is well worth the elimination of the paper lesson plan. Teachers who have done this kind of collaborative lesson planning report feeling a heightened sense of efficacy and professionalism. They appreciate the additional time set aside to plan and work with colleagues and they do not object to being held accountable for the results. Sharri's story is a good example.

"How come you made school so much more fun? I didn't know I was this smart." Statements like these make the challenges of our profession worth it, and the CIS makes statements like these much more likely to be said by students in our classrooms.

THE PICK-THREE STRATEGY

Governmental agencies typically categorize students by levels of performance. A common system is to identify students' performance as:

- Exceeds
- Meets
- Approaches
- Falls far below

This creates a numbers game because one criterion used to rank schools is the school's ability to move students from one category to a higher category. Consider the following as a strategy to help students achieve and also be successful in the numbers game.

During a faculty meeting ask each teacher to select a student in each of the lower three categories who is close to achieving at the next level and seems to just needs a boost. Ask each teacher to make the commitment to do what is necessary to get each of these students to the next level. Consider the impact if each of 30 or more teachers accomplishes this goal. This in no way suggests that the other students should be neglected in this process.

Remember the Effective Schools goal of learning for all. In fact, when teachers are successful in helping the selected students to improve their performance, it creates a sense of efficacy and teachers begin to ponder the question, "If I can help these three students be successful, how many more students can I help be successful?"

SHARRI'S STORY

Sharri was a member of a middle school language arts team. Prior to learning how to use the CIS, team members were frustrated with the lack of progress made by their English Language Learners. These students comprised 50 percent or more of each of their three classrooms. Because the students were not succeeding and they knew it, discipline was a serious problem. After four months of developing instructional calendars and common assessments, as well as meeting regularly to plan and assess their instruction, the team members were astounded at the results depicted on their data charts.

Sharri shared this mini-report at a staff meeting. "We want to share some very good news with you. In our three classrooms, discipline referrals are down 70 percent. We have reached the target in our formative academic mission statement and are adjusting it upwards. The best thing is what Fernando said to me yesterday. 'How come you made school so much more fun? I didn't know I was this smart.' We can't wait for student/parent conferences to share the specifics with the parents of our kids."

Chapter Nine

Formative Assessment

A TOOL FOR MONITORING STUDENT PROGRESS

There is a pervasive and ongoing discussion in the educational measurement community surrounding such terms as formative assessments, benchmark assessments, interim assessments, and summative assessments. We do not wish to enter into that discussion in this book but we do need to clarify how we use formative and summative in the Continuous Improvement System. Both of these measures are important. However, in the CIS we consider the data produced by formative assessment to be of greater value in the teaching and learning process than the summative data produced by end-of-year high-stakes tests.

We consider the end-of-year high-stakes test to be the ultimate summative assessment and agree to its importance in monitoring trends in the performance of previous students and for comparing data from state to state. This data is valuable for the policy makers, but not necessarily for the classroom teachers. In contrast, the purpose of formative assessments in the CIS is to provide teachers with "real-time" data that will help them effectively monitor the progress of their current students. It is this formative data that drives the instructional process.

In this chapter, we focus on formative assessment as a process and not a single event. We consider formative assessment to be the ongoing collection of real-time student achievement data from multiple sources. These sources include such things as formal paper-and-pencil tests, observations of students during a guided practice activity, or student work.

In the CIS, the formative assessment process yields data that are intended to:

- Help teachers identify areas where students are struggling and provide an appropriate intervention.
- Help students monitor their own progress, analyze their learning, and select more effective learning practices.

Because the data generated by the common assessments is so critical to the potential of the CIS, the rest of this chapter provides some suggestions about how to design, administer, and analyze the results of these important assessments.

THE COMMON ASSESSMENT TOOL

Common assessments are a critically important tool that teachers use in the formative assessment process. These are assessments that all teachers of a given grade level or subject area develop together and use to gather data about their students' learning. Common assessments help a teacher compile and analyze the performance data of individual students and the class as a whole. In addition, collecting and compiling the data from individual classrooms makes it possible for teachers of the same grade or subject area to analyze student performance data across an entire grade or subject area.

In the Continuous Improvement System, teachers develop these assessments at the same time they create the instructional calendar. This timing ensures that there is a direct alignment between what the teacher taught and what he assessed. When preparing the common assessment, teachers should construct two parallel versions of the test.

- The first version is used for the initial assessment to determine how well each student learned the content and/or skill of the lesson.
- The second version is used in the reteach/retest process to help students who did not master certain portions of the content or skill in the initial presentation. During this reteach/retest process, students receive additional instruction, learn from their mistakes, and take a retest on only those items they did not master initially.

There are some very important points to keep in mind when developing common formative assessments:

- The items should be grouped around a specific performance objective and the objective must be clearly identified. By grouping the items in this manner, teachers quickly become aware of the performance objectives where students are being successful and where students are struggling. The past practice of giving the test at the end of the chapter in the book without linking the test questions to an objective simply allowed teachers to determine a percentage of the correct answers and enter a grade in the grade book. However, this score gave no real indication of the students' understanding of any given objective.

- The items must match the content, format, and rigor of the state's high-stakes test.
- The items measuring new content should appear at the beginning of the assessment. The scores on these items are the only data included in the data charts described in the next chapter.
- A reduced number of review items are included on each assessment but scores for these items are not included in the charts. The review items are intended to encourage retention and provide information for the teacher regarding which students need remediation and on what content.

A multitude of resources are available to help teachers effectively create these assessments. Teachers may select items from the chapter test provided in the textbook. They may purchase items from web-based item banks or select from examples provided by the state. Teachers may also choose to write their own items. Whatever the source, it is important that the items are valid and that teachers are able to identify the specific performance objective that the item measures.

Carefully prepared test items give students an appropriate opportunity to demonstrate their knowledge of the content. One characteristic of a carefully prepared assessment is the number of test items the student must complete. As an example, in math, four test items per performance objective is optimal. Asking ten questions on a given performance objective will not provide the teacher with any more information than asking four questions. Lengthy assessments are frustrating for students, and they create additional work for teachers as they take longer to construct, administer, and grade.

We are often asked if there must be four questions administered for every performance objective identified in the state standards. The answer is no! The items on the common assessments should focus on the terminal objective. One example would be a terminal objective that requires students to add common fractions. There are several prerequisite objectives that must be mastered to accomplish this task. The student must know how to find a common denominator, adjust the numerators, and reduce a fraction to lowest terms, to name a few. These prerequisite objectives should be monitored in the classroom during the daily instruction. The items on the formative assessment consist of problems that require students to add

Table 9.1 Fourth-Grade Common Assessment Example

Division with a single-digit divisor—Solve one-variable equations
YOU MUST SHOW YOUR WORK IN ORDER TO RECEIVE CREDIT

New Content   S1-C2-PO6

1. Divide and find the quotient	2. Divide and find the quotient
$4\overline{)36}$	$723 \div 3$
A. 7	A. 271
B. 8	B. 260
C. 9	C. 240
D. 12	D. 241
3. Divide and find the quotient	4. If you have 15 cookies and you wish to give each of your 3 friends an equal share of cookies, how many cookies would you give to each friend?
112/2	
A. 51	
B. 61	A. 5
C. 60	B. 6
D. 56	C. 7
	D. None of the above

New Content   S3-C3-P3

5. Solve for the variable N:	6. Solve for the variable N:
$18 \div 3 = N$	$N + 7 = 13$
A. 5	A. 5
B. 6	B. 6
C. 7	C. 7
D. 9	D. 9
7. Solve for the variable N:	8. Solve for the variable N:
$18 - N = 13$	$N \times 3 = 0$
A. 5	A. 0
B. 6	B. 1
C. 7	C. 2
D. 9	D. 3

Review Content S1-C2-PO5

9. Multiply   27
              x 41

A. 68
B. 1107
C. 107
D. 27

common fractions. If they answer the questions correctly, the teacher can assume that students know the prerequisite skills. If they cannot, the teacher must conduct an error analysis to determine which prerequisite skills the students are missing.

As with the instructional calendar, a major benefit of the common formative assessments process is the dialogue that is generated among teachers. This dialogue leads teachers to a deeper understanding of the objective and provides the impetus for using new and innovative strategies.

The items in table 9.1 are in a multiple-choice format. This is not to imply that multiple choice is the mandated format for all items. However, since this is the most common format for many state test items in mathematics, using this format frequently ensures that students become familiar with it, and have the opportunity to practice and improve their test-taking skills.

ERROR ANALYSIS

Teachers often hand back test papers with a percentage score at the top and each item on the paper marked as correct or incorrect. Typically, after returning the tests, the teacher will ask, "Which problems do you want to see?" Then the teacher goes to the board and correctly works the requested problems. This is an unfortunate practice because the question and demonstration process does not give the teacher any data about what types of errors individual students are making nor the underlying causes of the errors. Knowledge about students' errors is vital information for teachers. This is true in every subject at every grade level.

Such knowledge creates a feedback loop that provides information regarding what each student does and does not understand at given points in the lesson. In the CIS, the teacher learns to use an error analysis form to gather information about each student's errors and about the clustering of errors made by groups of students in the class.

In order to demonstrate this process we will continue to use math examples. Errors in mathematics tend to fall into two basic categories. The first is a computational error such as multiplying 2 times 3 and answering 9. The second is a concept error where the student cannot form an equation after reading a word problem. By using an error analysis form like the one shown in table 9.2, the teacher can pinpoint the type of error each student is making on a given set of problems. The teacher fills in this form as individual student assessments are corrected. This process gives the teacher an important opportunity to carefully determine the exact error that each student has made.

Table 9.2   Error Analysis Form

PO and Error ➡ / Name ⬇	P O	Computation Error	Concept Error	P O	Computation Error	Concept Error	P O	Computation Error	Concept Error	P O	Computation Error	Concept Error	Error Description
Adam	1. 2. 6	1		3. 3. 3		4							36 ÷ 4 = 7 Equation solutions Multiply by 0
Bonita						1							Multiply by 0
Carl						1							Multiply by 0
Susan		3				4							Multiplication / division fact Equation solutions Multiply by 0

We suggest that teachers use this form at least three times to become familiar with the process. However, once teachers gain experience with the process they often find they no longer need the form because they develop their own shortcuts to obtaining and recording this data. We do suggest, however, that the form always be used if the scores on a given assessment are low for the class as a whole.

To enter the data into the error analysis form, follow these steps:

1. Enter the codes that indicate which state standards are being assessed (we refer to these as "performance objectives" or PO in the chart). These codes will vary from state to state. The individual at the district office with curriculum and/or assessment responsibilities is a good source for these codes if a school faculty is unfamiliar with them.
2. After correcting the tests, separate the students' papers into two groups: the students who met or exceeded the formative academic mission and those who did not. Enter the names of the students who met the formative

academic mission at the top of the form. Leave a space and enter the names of the students who did not meet the formative academic mission.

3. Record the number of computation and/or concept errors each student made in each group of items.

4. Identify the specific error in the error description section on the right side of the page.

In the example, we see that Adam made one computation error in the 1.2.6 performance objective (he divided 36 by 4 and came up with 7), but did the other three problems correctly. This is solid evidence that he knows how to do these problems and just made a careless error. However, in the 3.3.3 performance objective, he missed all four problems. This is a clear indication that he did not understand how to go about solving the equations. There is also a question about how well he understands the concept of multiplying by 0.

Bonita and Carl made no errors in the 1.2.6 performance objective. They both missed a question where they needed to multiply by 0.

Susan did not meet the academic mission and made three computation errors in the 1.2.6 performance objective. This would lead the teacher to question if she has a complete grasp of multiplication and division facts. She also missed all four items in the 3.3.3 performance objective. This demonstrates she does not understand how to solve equations and raises a question about her understanding of multiplying by 0.

The data recorded on the error analysis makes it clear that there were many errors by both students who met the formative academic mission and those who did not. The common errors appeared to be associated with solving the equations and multiplication by 0. At this point, the teacher must reflect upon the data and then search for ways to improve the effectiveness of his instruction on solving equations and multiplication by 0. By discussing this formative assessment data in a meeting of the instructional team, colleagues have an opportunity to offer ideas and support. If the teacher in our example has a colleague who had no student errors in equations and multiplication by 0, this colleague can be a source of suggestions and provide some peer coaching to the teacher who is having trouble teaching these concepts.

With this information in hand, the teacher is now prepared to plan the process for this unit in a way that adjusts the lesson to address the learning needs of all students. The teacher also can have discussions with individual students about the errors they have made.

Of course, if all the students reach the academic mission, there is no need for such a discussion. The teacher proceeds to the next lesson. However, it is unlikely that all students will realize this level of success at the end of the first teaching episode. In the past when some students were successful and others were not, teachers did one of two things. One, the teacher moved on and the learning gap between the successful students and the unsuccessful students expanded. Two, the teacher taught the lesson again, just the way he taught it the first time and usually to the whole class. The latter approach made little difference in student learning. The students who "got it" the first time again passed with flying colors, and those who did not do well improved minimally or not at all.

The Continuous Improvement System changes all that because it helps teachers do something different when they reteach the lesson. As a result of the common assessments, a teacher has data about which students understand the assessed concepts and skills and he can identify the specific errors that each student made. At this point the teacher can reteach the concepts and/or skills to the students who need additional assistance.

One of the major advantages of formative assessments in the CIS is that they not only allow the teacher to specifically help students who did not meet the formative academic mission, they also give the teacher a way to approach the students who did meet it but still made errors. The teacher could go to Bonita and Carl and say, "Even though you both met the academic mission, you both made a mistake. I know that you can do this correctly, so let's be sure you understand how to correct the mistake and then you can take the retest and gain a score that better reflects your true ability." This type of interchange helps students become adept at learning from their mistakes. As a result, both their competence and their confidence as learners increase.

THE RETEACH/RETEST PROCESS

For far too long, teachers have subjected students to the "teach-test-move on" process of instruction. This was the way teachers were taught when they were students and, until recently, it was the way they were taught to teach. This type of instruction is not in keeping with the spirit and intent of the No Child Left Behind legislation because moving on without addressing the students who did not learn the content definitely results in leaving those students behind. Neither is this process of instruction acceptable under the Effective Schools philosophy, which stresses that all children have an innate desire to learn and will learn if the adults who teach them pay attention to what, when, and how they teach the content. This demands that we provide students with additional support when they struggle with the content.

The "teach-test-move on" practice did save some time and probably allowed teachers to cover more content. Unfortunately, "covered" is the correct word. The content was not thoroughly taught and it was not accurately understood by many of the students. Students were exposed to a broad curriculum with little depth. The uncomplimentary description of this curriculum was, "a mile wide and an inch deep." This approach to teaching left many students with gaps in their learning. Unfortunately, these gaps created a ripple effect as students attempted to learn new and more advanced content without mastering the critical prerequisite skills. For some students failure became the norm, and for far too many, so did mediocre learning.

If our schools are to prepare students to meet the challenges of today's world, teachers must take the time to carefully analyze student work, understand the errors students are making, and ensure that students learn from their errors and correct them. This requires that schools develop effective procedures to assist students who didn't learn a concept or skill the first time. This is a significant shift in our teaching practice and has the potential to greatly increase the number of students succeeding as learners.

There are many approaches to the practice of reteach/retest. We suggest the following concepts be applied to any specific process that is selected to accomplish an effective reteach/retest:

- Students who do not attain scores that meet or exceed the formative academic mission should be given no option. They must be involved in the reteach/retest process.
- Students who achieve scores that meet or exceed the formative academic mission should be strongly encouraged to retake the test in an effort to attain a higher score. This allows students to correct careless errors and/or to demonstrate that they now understand a concept that was not previously understood.
- It is not always necessary to have students retake the entire parallel assessment. This can become a disincentive as students may feel punished by having to redo problems they have already done correctly. It is common to have the students take only the portion of the test associated with the items they missed on the initial assessment.
- Students should record their own scores on the initial tests and the retests. They do this on the individual data charts discussed in the next chapter. When students record their own scores, they tend to take more responsibility for the learning. The great majority of students are motivated by any visible increase they see on their individual chart. Teachers can enhance this sense of achievement by congratulating individuals and the entire class for their additional effort.

SEAN'S STORY

Sean was a student who was struggling in science. He would get sick to his stomach when it was time for a science test. Early in the year his teacher starting doing what Sean described as "this new testing thing." In his words, "When I blew a question, I knew which question because I entered my own stuff on my own chart. I also knew the teacher would help me learn how I blew it so I wouldn't do it again. Then I got to take the test over—a new one but sort of the same and on the same stuff. My grades are going up and up and up. My goal now is to get a hundred and I know I can do it!"

Not only did Sean knew he could do it, but his teacher did, too. More importantly, his classmates also knew it. They started cheering him on and working with him during lunch when he was struggling with an assignment. This was quite a change from the unkind teasing he had received in the past. Sean's experience in this classroom provided solid evidence that the culture of this high school was changing.

QUARTERLY ASSESSMENTS

Many districts use quarterly assessments to monitor how well students are being prepared for the high-stakes test in the fourth quarter of the year. We think it is time to give careful consideration to the content of such an assessment and the type of data produced.

In the Continuous Improvement System, we propose an approach that gives teachers additional real-time data concerning student achievement. In the curriculum chapter, teachers were directed to divide the curriculum into thirds—one-third to be taught in each of the first three quarters of the school year to prepare students for the high-stakes test that occurs in the fourth quarter.

When a school follows this schedule, it makes sense to construct a first-quarter assessment that measures only the content taught in the first quarter. This provides a clear indication of how well students have learned what was actually taught. The second-quarter test should consist primarily of items measuring student performance on the second-quarter curriculum, with two additional types of items included.

- First, a few items should monitor the retention of critical knowledge from the first quarter.
- Second, additional items should also be included to monitor the impact of the remediation effort on items that many students struggled with on the

first-quarter test. This spiraling pattern continues in the third quarter. The data collected over the first three quarters of the year should be used to drive instruction during the weeks in the fourth quarter prior to the high-stakes test.

One model that is frequently used is an end-of-course test given at the end of each quarter as a predictor of student performance on the high-stakes test. The end-of-course test model may, at best, give district-level personnel a preliminary indication of how students will perform on the high-stakes test, but the resulting general data usually produces little information of real value to the classroom teacher. If the teacher is willing to dig into the item analysis and weed out the questions associated with content that has actually been taught, they may find some valuable data. However, this is often confusing and time consuming.

More than likely, this scenario will set up a very discouraging situation for both students and teachers. Logically, if the students have learned all that they should have learned during the first quarter, a high score should be somewhere around 25 percent correct. We suggest it will be difficult to convince students that knowing one quarter of the answers is a successful performance on a test!

Think about the environment that the end-of-course format creates. As students sit with pencils poised, listening to directions about the test, they will often hear a statement like this: "Don't be concerned if you encounter something on the test that you don't know. That just means that I have not taught it yet. We will learn about it later. Just do your best." This has to be a frustrating message to the learner. Does anyone really believe this situation is consistent with high expectations or that it motivates students to do their best?

Principals and teachers must define why they are administering these tests. If the intent is to collect data that will be used to improve both teacher performance and student achievement, better information is generated when students are tested on content that they have actually been taught as opposed to testing them on content that they may or may not have been taught.

In districts where the end-of-course format is used the following question is often raised: "Does the data from the common assessments administered in the classroom predict student performance on the quarterly assessments?" This is a great question with a rather complex answer. That answer is maybe. Consider the following:

- The common assessments that are used in the classroom are measures of current student performance. The end-of-course quarterly assessments are predictors of future performance.

- The common assessments that are used in the classroom test students on content that they have been taught. The end-of-course quarterly assessments test students on content that they have been taught and content that they have not been taught.
- Because of the differences identified in the first two bullets, we can only guess if the data from the two assessments correlate during the school year. The high-stakes test at the end of the year does test students over content that they have been, or at least should have been, taught. This data should be highly correlated with the classroom assessments if the principal and faculty members have implemented the CIS with fidelity.
- If teachers have taught the required performance objectives, created common assessments that are directly linked to the required performance objectives, created common assessments in the same format and with the same rigor as the high-stakes test, and taught students not only the content but the reasoning skills required to answer the questions, the classroom and grade-level data charts discussed in chapter 10 will be accurate predictors of students' future performance.

Currently, schools are buried in data on a variety of topics. We recognize that each piece of the data is important to someone. However, the CIS is dedicated to producing only on-time student achievement data that teachers can immediately use to enhance the opportunity for all students to be successful.

A PRINCIPAL'S STORY

A principal invited Fred to his office to review the data from the high-stakes. The principal recalled how, three years earlier, teachers were functioning independently—even competitively—and the academic scores were barely meeting the expected standard.

He showed Fred a PowerPoint presentation that he prepared for the opening faculty meeting. The slides recounted the goals that were set and how each goal was accomplished. One of the primary goals was to successfully implement the instructional team structure. The final slides celebrated the fact that the school was now achieving higher academic scores than in the past and had met AYP. He told the story of a student who had struggled for several years and was now achieving well. He spoke of several classrooms where no student was now considered to be failing.

As he spoke, the emotion overtook him and the tears began to flow. He said, "I'm so proud of what we have done for these kids. When I show this to the faculty, there will not be a druy eye in the place—obviously including mine."

Chapter Ten

Student Achievement Data

MONITORING PROGRESS TOWARD
THE ACADEMIC MISSION

Accurate, real-time data is the lifeblood of any organization's effort to improve performance. This is especially true in education, where teaching and learning activities must be continuously monitored and improved to ensure that every student learns at his maximum capacity.

In the Continuous Improvement System, teachers generate this essential data by conducting common formative assessments that they have created with their "job-alike" colleagues at the end of each instructional unit. The data from the assessments are public information and are displayed in a clear, user-friendly visual format. This makes it possible for anyone at any time to evaluate and compare the current level of performance in any classroom to the level of performance identified in the formative academic mission. The CIS uses three simple charts to track data:

1. The Classroom Performance Chart depicts the performance of the classroom as a whole. This chart is maintained by the teacher.
2. The Student Performance Chart provides students with an effective way to track their individual progress. The students maintain their own charts.
3. The Grade-level (or Content-area) Performance Chart shows the level of achievement across an entire grade level or subject area. This is maintained by the facilitator of the instructional team.

These charts provide an accurate picture of current performance and progress toward achieving both the summative and formative academic mission.

The data are presented in bar graph form because this format is easy for students, educators, and parents to understand.

CLASSROOM PERFORMANCE DATA

In the initial work with the CIS, we attempted to have teachers create the classroom performance chart by using Excel™ or PowerPoint™. However, this proved to be a very frustrating and unproductive endeavor. We now ask teachers to use a paper copy of the chart and highlighter pens to color in the data. It is not "high tech," but it works because it is faster and not dependent on a teacher's knowledge of computer programs.

We suggest that all teachers in the school use the same two colors of highlighters, and in response to this suggestion, they often choose their school's colors. The first color is used to represent the initial assessment data and the second represents the data after the reteach/retest process. The contrasting colors clearly show the proportional relationship of these two measures. A third color should be used to record the district's quarterly assessment data. These three contrasting colors create a vivid image of how students are performing on the school and district assessments. This chart is posted in every classroom next to the instructional calendar. This allows anyone who enters a classroom to very quickly determine what content has been taught and how well the students mastered that content.

Figure 10.1 shows an example of how the chart is used.

In this example we see:

- The first column represents the vision to have all students completely master the curriculum. As we have previously discussed, this is not reasonable and attainable, but the pursuit of the unattainable is an effective catalyst to improve performance.
- The bold line that appears at the 80 percent level represents the formative academic mission we discussed in chapter 6. Recall that our academic mission specified that 80 percent of the students would score at or above 75 percent correct.
- The date of the assessment appears at the top of the entry. The assessment number, a brief description, and the performance objective are listed below the date entry. This ensures clear tracking of any given performance objective from the calendar, and allows the faculty to quickly coordinate the curriculum information from the instructional calendar with student achievement data.
- The second column represents Assessment #1 and shows 19 out of 25 students (76 percent) initially achieved at or above the 75 percent correct response level that was set in the academic mission. This is 4 percent below

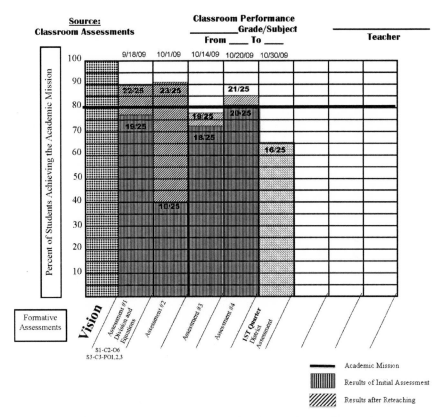

Figure 10.1   Classroom Assessments—Percent of Students Achieving the Academic Mission

our goal. The fraction 19/25 is placed at the top of the column. This fraction will later be used in the creation of the grade-level chart.

- The retest data is added to the top of the column. Here, 22 of the 25 students (88 percent) achieved at or above the 75 percent correct level. This is 8 percent above the academic mission level. The fraction is also used in creating the grade-level chart. It is important to depict the final level of achievement on the chart, because the impact of seeing the increase in scores is a powerful intrinsic motivator for both the teacher and the students.
- The third column (Assessment #2) shows that only 10 of 25 students met the academic mission on the initial assessment but that 23 of 25 students met the academic mission following the activity. This is a clear indication that the students simply were not ready to take the initial assessment.
- The inclusion of the retest data on the chart allows for a quick assessment of the effectiveness of the reteach/retest process employed by the teacher. For example, the fourth column (Assessment #3) shows that the class did not meet the

academic mission even after the reteach/retest. Based on this data, we may conclude that the reteaching was ineffective. This requires the teacher to carefully
analyze his instruction and make plans to revisit this section of the curriculum.

- The fifth column (Assessment #4) again shows that the reteaching was
  ineffective and also highlights a trend in the data. The final achievement
  levels across all four assessments are very similar. This should prompt the
  teacher to question whether it is the same students who are not meeting the
  academic mission and, if so, are in need of a formal intervention. This may
  be a topic of discussion at an instructional team meeting.

Maintaining this data over the entire school year provides valuable information when it is time for the final review prior to the high-stakes test. It is also
important to be able to compare the data from year to year. A pattern of low
scores from a given classroom or grade level/subject may be cause for concern.
Looking at the performance of a given group of students in the preceding year
can isolate an issue specific to a given classroom, grade level, or subject.

The classroom performance chart also includes data from the district's
quarterly assessments. In this example, 16 of the 25 students attained the desired level of achievement. This is below the classroom scores on the school's
common assessments. On its own, this piece of information is only a signal to
look for a trend in the second- and third-quarter district assessment scores. If
those scores show a pattern that is consistently above or below the school's
common assessment scores, the validity and level of difficulty of either or
both sets of assessment instruments must be evaluated.

The classroom performance chart is the primary tool used during meetings
of the instructional teams. Members of the grade-level/subject area team examine the data on their individual charts and compare and contrast the results.
The objective of the dialogue during the meeting is collaborating to ensure
that every student reaches the performance target indicated in the formative
academic mission. Teachers look at the data to identify problem areas common to all classrooms and consider instructional strategies that might address
identified problems. If one teacher's chart shows that many of his students did
not meet the performance target, that teacher uses the members of his instructional team as collegial problem solvers. They work together to come up with
instructional strategies that the teacher could try with struggling learners.

STUDENT PERFORMANCE DATA

When students record their own data, they begin to understand the value of assessment and the information it produces. As students fill in their own charts,

they learn to take pride in their progress. They also learn how to learn from their mistakes and come to realize their own active role in the student/teacher partnership. The student performance chart is also a valuable tool in communicating with parents about student performance. The chart can be used during parent-teacher conferences or sent home regularly for parent review.

Teachers find many inventive ways to help students to maintain their charts. One way is to give each student a pocket or file folder with the blank chart enclosed. Students enter their data following each assessment. The actual assessment can also be kept in the file for use during parent conferences. More mature students may be able to keep the file in their possession. The teacher may want to keep the files of younger students and distribute them when data needs to be entered. This chart is a private student record and other students should not have access to the chart.

Primary elementary teachers may have concerns about the ability of these very young students to enter data on a chart. However, we have observed that when the teacher gives a clear demonstration of what to do and then carefully monitors the activity, young students can successfully fill in their charts. Although the first attempts by students may be a bit messy, they will improve with time and practice.

Figure 10.2 shows what an individual student chart may look like.

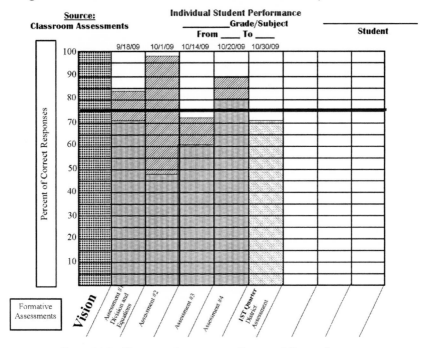

Figure 10.2   Classroom Assessments—Percent of Correct Responses

In this example we can see that:

- The bold line that appears at the 75 percent level represents the formative academic mission we discussed in chapter 6.
- The date appears at the top of the column and the assessment content is recorded below the column. It is not necessary for students to identify the state standard code.
- In this example, the student's scores for both the initial assessment and the re-test are shown. The student's performance on the district test is also shown.

The chart may be used with students to encourage reflection and goal setting. Ask students:

- In what units were you most successful?
- What caused you to have this success? (Consider both in-class and out-of-class activity.)
- In what units did you have the most difficulty?
- What caused you to struggle in these units? (Consider both in-class and out-of-class activity.)
- What would you like to achieve in the next several weeks?
- What will help you the most as you work to achieve your goal?

ROSA'S STORY

This beautiful little girl was a third-grade student who had struggled through the first and second grades. Her difficulty with the English language and her complete lack of study skills had greatly inhibited her academic progress.

Rosa's third-grade teacher was part of an instructional team implementing the Continuous Improvement System. This meant Rosa was now recording her progress on what she had learned during a given lesson. By mid-year, it had become evident that Rosa's experience with an organized system of data collection and analysis was beginning to help her make significant academic progress. Her skills with the English language were also improving.

During a visit to Rosa's classroom, Fred was talking with students and asking them to explain their individual data charts to him. When he came to Rosa, she informed him that she did not have her chart. He asked the obvious question inquiring as to its whereabouts. With a broad smile on her face, she told him that she had taken the chart home to show her parents and her mother was so pleased that she taped the chart on the refrigerator door and would not give it back to her.

The teacher happily made a new chart for Rosa.

Two of the most powerful aspects of the Continuous Improvement System are the partnership the teacher and the student form as they record and use the data, and the ownership students develop around the responsibility and success that they experience.

GRADE-LEVEL PERFORMANCE DATA

The grade-level performance chart is the primary tool used during meetings of the leadership team. This data gives the leadership team visual information on how the students are performing across any given grade level and in the school as a whole. It provides information as to the effectiveness of the reteach/retest process. It also is used to determine if this is the time to adjust the formative academic mission to either a higher or a lower level. If so, the leadership team develops a plan for making this adjustment and presents the plan at a faculty meeting in the near future.

A typical grade-level performance chart will look like the example in figure 10.3.

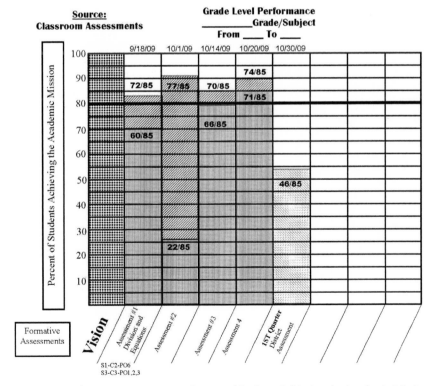

Figure 10.3   Classroom Assessments—Percent of Students Achieving the Academic Mission

In this example, we note the following:

- The formative academic mission is again represented by a bold line at the 80 percent level.
- The assessment number and the content are recorded below the column and again include the state codes. The date of the assessment is at the top of the data entry.
- The chart includes data indicating the level of performance of the entire grade level/subject on the district's quarterly assessment. This data must be monitored for trends that show school performance that is above or below the expected level.
- The facilitator for each instructional team develops this chart showing the level of achievement across an entire grade or subject area. To develop and maintain this chart, the instructional team facilitator collects the raw data from each classroom on the classroom data collection form.

When the grade-level facilitator uses the classroom data collection form, the data for a given assessment will look like the example in figure 10.4. Here are some important items to note in the example:

- The raw data from the classroom performance chart is entered into the grade-level performance chart. Here, a total of 58 students across the three classes met the academic mission requirement of 75 percent or more correct answers on Assessment #1. This is 68 percent of the total number of students (85).

_____ Grade & Subject   From ____ To ____

Data → Teacher ↓	1st Test	Re-test	1st Test	Re-test
Andrews	19/25	22/25		
Bennett	20/30			
Castillo	21/30	26/30		

Assessment #1
Divisions and
Equations

S1-C2-PO6
S3-C3-PO1,2,3

Figure 10.4   Classroom Data Collection Form

- There is no retest score entered for Bennett even though the academic mission was not met in the classroom (20 of 30 for 67 percent). If this becomes a pattern, the administration must investigate and correct this situation. If the reteach/retest process is implemented as intended, retest data should almost always appear on the form.
- The retest data from Andrews and Castillo shows that 8 additional students achieved the academic mission requirement and so we now have 48 of the 55 students in these two classes who have met the requirement (87 percent), but the grade-level data is inconclusive without Bennett's retest scores.

WHAT ABOUT READING?

In the introduction we stated that the CIS can be used effectively at any grade level and with any subject matter. In order to support that claim, we will demonstrate a couple of ways that the System can be used in the area of reading.

The Dynamic Indictors of Basic Early Literacy Skills (DIBELS) is a commonly used tool to measure reading skills in grades K–6. It is comprised of a developmental sequence of one-minute measures that grow progressively more difficult. Students undergo multiple assessments each year and may move among the three levels of benchmark, strategic, and intensive. DIBELS results can be used to evaluate individual student development and provide information relating to the effectiveness of the instruction they are receiving.

The DIBELS Analysis Chart gives teachers a way of collecting and using DIBELS data to drive instruction.

When the teacher completes this form, it will look like the example in table 10.1.

This example depicts data from a single classroom although the same form can be used to track data for a grade level, or even school wide. Note that scores are entered for only those students who have both prior and current scores.

Color coding the data makes it easy to monitor movement: black = maintained level, green = movement to a higher level, and red = movement to a lower level.

Let's look at what this data tells us:

- On the prior assessment, 28 students were tested with 20 achieving at the benchmark level, 6 at the strategic level, and 2 at the intensive level.
- On the current assessment, 16 of the students who previously scored at the benchmark level maintained that level of performance. Three of those students moved down one level to strategic, and one fell all the way to intensive.

Table 10.1   DIBELS Analysis

TEACHER _____   DATE _____

Students with both current and prior scores	Prior Score	Current Score			Percent Effective
	# of Students	Level Movement			
		Benchmark	Strategic	Intensive	
Benchmark	20	16	3	1	80%
Strategic	6	4	1	1	3%
Intensive	2	0	0	2	0%
Total	28	20	4	4	

% Effective is calculated by:

Benchmark = maintained ÷ prior total at this level
Strategic = maintained and moved to benchmark ÷ prior total at this level
Intensive = moved to strategic and/or benchmark ÷ prior total at this level

Students who maintained Benchmark Alex	Students who moved down to Strategic Bonita	Students who moved down to Intensive Carl
Students who moved up to Benchmark Diane	Students who maintained Strategic Eric	Students who moved down to Intensive Frank
Students who moved up to Benchmark	Students who moved up to Strategic	Students who maintained Intensive Gale

- The names of the students are entered into the lower grid and teachers use this specific information to monitor performance and target individual students for assistance.
- The percentage effective data is a general indicator of how effective the instruction has been in maintaining or improving student performance. This type of data is not to be used as teacher evaluation. However, it is an

indicator that may cause an evaluator to observe the instruction in a class-room. This is especially true if low scores become a pattern.

- This data is calculated as follows:
Benchmark - maintained ÷ total at the prior level (16 / 20 = 80 percent)
Strategic - maintained + moved to benchmark ÷ total at the prior level (1+4 / 6 = 83 percent)
Intensive - moved to strategic + moved to benchmark ÷ total at the prior level (0 / 2 = 0 percent)

All of the philosophy and procedures in the CIS remain the same. The data that is collected simply looks different.

Reading content is significantly different from math content. In math, there is a sequence of many specific skills that must be mastered. In reading, there are a limited number of skills that are cycled throughout the process. Examples of some of the major reading skills include comprehension, main idea, inference, and drawing conclusions. It is typical practice to assess reading by having students read a passage and then answer a series of questions associated with the skills. Teachers usually include questions associated with all the major skills on a single assessment. This is not helpful to the teacher or the students, as it does not zero in on a specific skill. Even though the student will be using all the skills mentioned previously, the teacher should emphasize some of them and then test the students' mastery of those skills.

We have observed teachers intentionally focus on one skill at a time and create common assessments that we believe offer an approach that results in more effective data. Since the teachers considered comprehension as the bottom-line skill, they included a significant number of questions associated with this skill on every assessment. They also included a significant number of questions on a specific second skill in any given assessment. In order to monitor retention and progress on a skill that students may have struggled with in the past, teachers included a limited number of questions on selected content on every assessment. The teachers enter the data from the two major skills on the same data chart template that was used to monitor math data. This format makes the data look the same as the math data. This chart is posted in the classroom beside the math data chart.

A reading chart would look like the example in figure 10.5.

In this chart we see:

- The first assessment primarily focused on the skills of comprehension and main idea.
- The second assessment primarily focused on the skills of comprehension and inference.

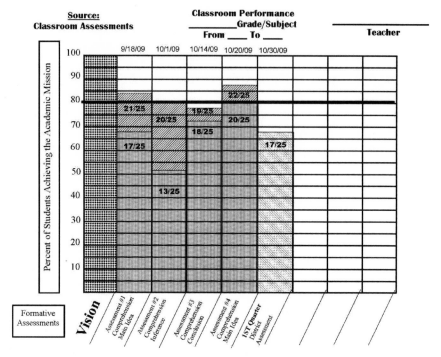

Figure 10.5   Classroom Assessments—Percent of Students Achieving the Academic Mission

- The third assessment primarily focused on the skills of comprehension and conclusion.
- The fourth assessment mirrored the first and again primarily focused on the skills of comprehension and main idea. This data indicates that there has been a gain from the first assessment. In the fourth assessment, 20 of 25 students met the academic mission on the initial assessment as opposed to only 17 of 25 in the first assessment. The gain is also seen in the reteach/retest data.
- The first-quarter district assessment indicates that 17 of 25 students met expectations. This assessment covered all reading skills and provides an indication of how students would likely perform on the high-stakes test administered at the end of the year.

TEACHER USE OF DATA

We firmly believe that data are problem-identifying tools and not problem-solving tools. Careful analysis of data can tell educators where a problem exists but it is then up to the educators to find and implement solutions.

In an effort to identify problems, political and district office officials often separate data by student's race, gender, and socioeconomic status. We accept that this practice is valuable to these individuals as they take a global view of student achievement. In the Continuous Improvement System, we believe that this data is of little or no use to the classroom teacher.

The classroom teacher must simply identify two groups of students: those who have met the academic mission and those who have not. This is problem identification. The teacher enters the problem-solving part of the process by asking:

- How do I challenge the students who are achieving well above the academic mission?
- How do I prevent the students who are achieving just above the academic mission from falling behind?
- How can I best assist the students who are not achieving the academic mission?

The classroom teacher should not be concerned with the student's race, gender, and socioeconomic status. The only concern of the teacher must be assisting all students to perform at the highest level of their ability.

SPECIAL EDUCATION STUDENTS

The CIS is based on the vision that learning is for all students, and this includes special education students. In fact, the objective-based individual education plan (IEP) with related assessments is an excellent example of the accountability factor that drives this System.

In many cases (such as self-contained students with profound disabilities), the IEP objectives are not aligned to grade-level standards. The state expectations for learning for these students are explicit and assessed continuously. The students in resource programs for less severe disabilities are expected to master grade-level skills. The difference is that they will need more time and more assistance to achieve these skills.

The CIS was not originally designed for the special education classroom. However, that does not mean special education students are ignored by the System. The exclusion of special education students would violate the "learning for all" vision of Effective Schools. Many special education students are mainstreamed into standard classrooms and the System can effectively be used to support them. While some special education students will never be able to perform at the level set forth in the academic mission, the System is designed to help them perform at their highest possible level.

Early in this book, we discussed the critical need for teams of teachers to work in collaboration. We believe that this is so vital that we urged schools to make this a requirement. This is especially true of the classroom teacher and the special education teacher. Clear communication and a joint effort between these two educators are essential to the success of their shared students.

When teachers are in the early stages of using the CIS, they tend to worry that low student achievement scores will reflect negatively on their abilities as a teacher. They often express concern about how their classroom scores are impacted by the special education students in their room. Some may even seek ways to have special education students transferred out of their class. This concern will diminish as teachers gain experience with the System and develop trust in each other and their administrators. Until that time, leaders of the school need to be keenly aware of the potentially destructive nature of this competitive phase and take appropriate actions to alleviate teachers' concerns. This may be a situation where the speaking from the head/speaking from the heart process can be helpful (see the appendix).

Very early in the school year, the district-level director of the special education program (or other appropriate administrator) should meet with the entire faculty to review the laws and district policies that govern the special education program. Everyone must be fully aware of the legal requirements and the accommodations that can be made for special education students. All educators in the district need to clearly understand that the IEP drives the education of the special education student.

To best address the needs of special education students while using the CIS, we make the following suggestions:

- The instructional teams are at the very core of the System and the special education teacher must be a key member of the team. Time must be set aside for special education teachers to meet with instructional teams to discuss the instructional calendar, review the common assessments, and identify strategies that are most appropriate for individual students.
- When assigning students to special education teachers, group the students by grade level. Whenever possible, assign all students from a given grade level to a specific special education teacher or team of special education teachers. The special education teacher should review the IEP of each student with the classroom teacher. This will foster more open communication that will result in a joint plan for the student.
- If it is appropriate under the IEP, the special education teacher can administer the common assessment and make specific accommodations to ensure the student is afforded the best possible opportunity to demon-

strate his knowledge. If the student has an IEP for reading and is taking a test in math, the teacher may read the directions and the word problems to the student.

- Special education teachers should look for grade-level content that can be learned without dependency on a prerequisite skill. For example, a fourth-grade student can learn the names of geometric shapes even if he has not mastered all the addition and subtraction facts. Ensuring that students master some specific grade-level skills will elevate the students' performance on the high-stakes test. It will also enhance the student's view of himself as a learner.

How the special education students' test scores are entered on the data charts is a delicate issue. In the CIS it is important to avoid any type of embarrassing or demoralizing situation for any student. Many teachers have expressed concern for students who must consistently enter low scores on the data charts. These students already know that they are struggling and the absence or presence of the data chart does not change that basic fact. We ask that you keep in mind the "learning for all" vision and the purpose of the CIS: to create a culture in which each teacher provides high-quality instruction and each student performs at the highest level his individual ability will allow. Teachers must use the charts to provide a realistic picture to students and their parents and to celebrate every success for these students regardless of the size of the success.

In the end, most special education students will be required to take the high-stakes test and most likely few accommodations will be made for them. If the teacher and the leadership of the school are to have an overall accurate picture of how the student body as a whole is performing, scores achieved by special education students must be included on the classroom chart. If teachers so desire, a second chart that eliminates the scores of the special education students may also be maintained. This will be a more accurate indicator of how the non–special education students are performing. This second chart is for teacher use only and must not be posted in the classroom.

The same procedure of creating the first two charts may be used for the grade-level/subject chart. Again, only the chart that includes all students should be displayed and only the leadership team should be privy to charts that exclude special education data.

The special education teacher may be best prepared to deal with the student when it is time to enter the data on the student's individual data chart. This can be done in a setting that is more private than the regular classroom. This allows the teacher and the student to have a more productive dialogue. This chart also is a valuable tool to be used during parent conferences.

Chapter Eleven

Accountability

EFFECTIVE USE OF INFORMAL AND
FORMAL ACCOUNTABILITY

Teachers and administrators are expected to perform as professionals. We believe that statement begs the question, "What does it mean to be a professional?" In our opinion, a professional is someone who knows the job, knows what has to be done to do the job, and holds himself and his colleagues accountable for doing the job well. This definition makes the strong point that accountability is an integral component of being a professional. The focus of this chapter is how the Continuous Improvement System employs a clear understanding and skillful use of accountability as an effective way to improve teacher performance.

People tend to want to do their work effectively and they find being held accountable to do so both appropriate and motivating. In *The Motivation to Work* (1993), Frederick Herzberg discussed factors affecting job attitudes and performance. When he surveyed workers they reported that what they wanted from supervisors was to be given a job and allowed to find the best way to accomplish that job. They appreciated the feeling of being trusted to do the job well and did not mind being held accountable to do so. As a result, he concluded that a sense of achievement, the personal knowledge that you have performed a job well, was the most powerful factor leading to a sense of job satisfaction.

There are two essential elements in any successful change process. Accountability is one. The other element is clarity of expectations. If both of these elements are present, the change process has a very strong chance of succeeding. When a change process is being implemented in a school it is initially the responsibility of the principal to ensure that the elements of accountability and clear expectations are present. The word *initially* is of particular importance. The principal begins this work, but eventually everyone in the organization must share responsibility for being clear about expectations and be willing to hold themselves and each other accountable for their fulfillment.

In this chapter we describe how the superintendent, designated central office administrators, and principals build a shared responsibility for individual and group accountability that is an integral factor in the successful implementation of the entire System. When both informal and formal accountability are embedded in the culture of the district and the school, educational professionals hold themselves and each other accountable for achieving the academic mission.

HOW IS INFORMAL ACCOUNTABILITY USED IN THE CIS?

Informal accountability is the result of knowing what is expected, knowing how well you are doing what is expected, and holding yourself accountable for continuously meeting or exceeding the expectation. The power of informal accountability was clearly described in a January 26, 2009, article in the *Arizona Republic* newspaper. The article described how Coach Ken Whisenhunt changed the culture of the Arizona Cardinals football team by demanding dedication, accountability, and consistency from the players. Demanding that these expectations be met changed the team from being perennial losers to playing in the Super Bowl in just two seasons. Player Sean Morey spoke about the impact of that change in the team culture when he described his personal experience while watching game films. "Watching the film, you sometimes have this voice; you can hear it in your head. When things go wrong, it says: It's not OK—it's not OK!" He was a team member who was holding himself and his teammates accountable for the quality of their performance.

With the CIS, this same powerful internal dialogue begins to go on inside teachers' heads when they review classroom data with colleagues. When teachers work in instructional teams looking at their individual classroom and collective team data, they will notice that some students are not succeeding. It could be just one student, several students in one teacher's class, or a trend across many students in several or all of the classrooms. Regardless of the magnitude of the problem, when they see it, clear expectations and accountability are in play if you hear them say, "This is not working. It is not acceptable. What are we going to do to change this?"

There are two important considerations about such statements. One is that teachers see the problem and identify it as an opportunity and not as criticism.

The other is that teachers see the success of all students as their collective professional responsibility. This is a major culture shift from the mindset of "my classroom and my students" to "our students."

It is human nature to want to perform competently, and the informal accountability that is inherent within the CIS makes valuable use of this human tendency. You will know that the culture of your school is changing for the better when you hear a teacher say, "The scores are not where I want them to be. The students just are not there yet. I know they can and will get there. What ideas do you have to help me help them raise their scores on the formative assessments?" This is informal accountability in action.

To best understand the role of informal accountability, put yourself in the place of a teacher who is involved in the System. What feelings would you experience if the principal or a visitor to the school entered your classroom and began to look at the instructional calendar and the classroom data chart posted on the wall? What feelings would you experience if you met with your peers in an instructional team meeting, displayed your classroom data chart, and discussed the level of student achievement in your class? What would you experience emotionally if you participated in a faculty meeting and your grade-level/subject chart was displayed and discussed? Would these emotional responses challenge you in a very positive way to consistently put forth your best effort? Our experience with the System is that in time, the answer to this last question for the overwhelming number of teachers will be, "Absolutely!" It does not happen overnight, but it does happen.

When the result of a teacher's work becomes public in the form of a classroom data chart, there is a natural desire to have the data demonstrate a high level of professional competence. When these data are connected to the faces of students, the teacher is highly motivated to do everything possible to ensure that each student succeeds. When student achievement data are considered across a grade level or content area, this collective data helps the members of the instructional team more clearly name and problem solve issues that are interfering with student learning. Frequently, the problem solving generated by informal accountability among the team members motivates them to seek out and participate in professional development experiences that help them develop and use more effective instructional skills.

When teachers collaborate to develop the instructional calendars and common assessments, informal accountability is present. Each teacher wants to contribute to the success of the team as a whole. They want the quality of the work to positively impact the learning of all the students at that grade level or in that content area. If any individual gets data that indicates he is not meeting the expectations of the organization, the informal accountability helps tune in that voice in his head that says, "It's not OK."

The strong sense of informal accountability generated by the CIS results in this individual accepting the personal responsibility to do whatever is necessary to make it OK.

Informal accountability plays a major role in data analysis, construction of instructional calendars, and the development of common assessments. It also positively affects the quality and productivity of faculty meetings. Consider the potential impact on the faculty if the principal:

- Asks an individual teacher to share something that he recently did that demonstrates one of the core commitments or the school vision.
- Asks an individual teacher to share an instructional strategy that resulted in improved student learning.
- Asks a grade-level or content-area team to share how a student learning problem that existed in most of their classrooms was solved.
- Asks a grade-level or content-area team to bring to a faculty meeting a problem they have not succeeded in solving and ask the faculty to brainstorm some possible solutions. A case study protocol can be helpful and we have included an example in the appendix.
- Asks a teacher or a team to demonstrate an instructional strategy that can be used at all grade levels or content areas.
- Asks a grade-level or content-area team to bring a proposal for professional development where the content and skill set of the training would apply at all grade levels and/or across all content areas.
- Asks a group of students to attend a faculty meeting and discuss how the CIS has helped them. They may identify such things as the impact of the classroom and student data charts or how they learned from their mistakes during the reteach/retest process. This can also be done during a parent meeting, a district-level meeting, or even at a governing board meeting.

The misuse or avoidance of informal accountability often results in the maintenance of the status quo or even a decline in the quality of performance. If a school is performing poorly, the teachers may begin to engage in nonproductive practices like blaming and defending. In that instance, people's internal voices aren't saying, "It's not OK." Instead, they are saying, "It's not my fault," "The assessment is too difficult," "The district office is being unreasonable," "Our kids can't learn at this level," "There is not enough time." None of these statements are productive and when they become the norm, the effect is inevitably destructive. School leaders must prevent this defensive theme from becoming "the way we do business" in the school. Principals and faculty members can help make informal accountability a consistent part of their practice if:

- The leaders of the organization make expectations explicitly clear. What is expected? Why is it expected? When is it expected, and of whom?
- Leaders check to make sure the receiver of the expectations has the same understanding of the expectation as the leader.
- Leaders and team members review the expectations on a regular basis.
- Everyone celebrates when expectations are successfully met.
- Colleagues engage in problem solving and generate new ways to meet expectations.
- Everyone learns to respectfully hold themselves and each other accountable for meeting the expectations.
- Teachers teach students about informal accountability and help them learn to hold themselves accountable for meeting the academic mission.
- Parents are informed about the expectations the school has for their student, how students will be held accountable, and how they can help the student to succeed.

HOW IS FORMAL ACCOUNTABILITY USED IN THE CIS?

The district's teacher evaluation system is the primary tool used to hold individuals formally accountable for the quality of their work, and these evaluation systems are often described as having two purposes. The first is to hold people accountable for their performance and to make job status decisions. The second is to improve performance. These purposes are not mutually exclusive, but the inevitable intermingling of the two can be troublesome. It is important for school administrators to fully understand the two distinct roles of evaluator and coach. The ability to appropriately function in these roles has a powerful impact on the administrator's relationship with the faculty.

The principal never uses the data depicted on the classroom data charts in teacher evaluation. There are far too many variables involved to make a formal judgment about a teacher's competence based solely on this type of data. However, the charts may give a clear signal that a visit to a teacher's classroom is appropriate. Decisions about teacher competency at the formal accountability level should only be made based on firsthand observations over time.

In the role of either evaluator or coach, the quality of the data collected and the feedback provided by the administrator is crucial to effecting positive change in a person's performance. Above all, the feedback must be an accurate reflection of current performance. Unfortunately, this is not what happens in many situations. Jan Halper reported on a ten-year study of this condition in her book, *Quiet Desperation: The Truth About Successful Men* (1989). She found that over 70 percent of evaluators saw themselves as "people pleasers" and said they lied about poor performance rather than tell subordinates the truth. This practice was found to be very counterproductive because the false feedback actually encouraged people to continue their incompetent behavior.

AN ACCOUNTABILITY STORY

Kaylene and Maria are principals of sister schools in Glendale, Arizona. They each implemented the Continuous Improvement System in their respective schools. They discovered that they were facing exactly the same issue, but with different grade levels. Although they took divergent approached, both successfully addressed the issue

Following the 2009 AIMS test, data for each school demostrated two clear patterns. First, in all grades but one, the number of students in the categories of "falling far below" and "approaching" was declining while the number of students in the "meets" and "exceeds" categories was growing significantly. These result were anticipated based on the classroom and grade-level data charts that had been ovserved during the school year.

When the principals examined cohort data, the second pattern emerged. In the grade level below the grade where the low scores became evident, the students scored well. In the grade above, the students again scored well. This clearly indicated that the issue existed at a single grade level.

Dr. Skoglund met individually with the principals to organize an agenda for a meeting with their instructional teams. It was crucial that the agendas revolved around problem solving, not blaming the teachers whose students had demonstrated a lack of progress. When the principals met with their respective instructional teams, they carefully communicated this purpose and they checked to be sure that the teachers understood what they were communicating.

Maria began her meeting by displaying and clearly explaining the data to the teachers. Then she asked the teachers to express their opinions and feelings about what the data depicted. The subsequent discussions started out somewhat emotional and defensive but eventually settled into productive dialogue concerning curriculum, instructional strategies, the need to work collaboratively, and plans to ovserve other instructional teams.

Kaylene gave the data to her teachers and asked them to bring plans for addressing the issue to a meeting. The teachers took this opportunity to engage in self-reflection and came to the meeting with some very solid ideas as to how to change the focus of their instruction and make better use of time.

In each case, the teachers knew that they had been held accountable for the level of student achievement in their classrooms and because of the respectful and collaborative manner in which the principals conveyed their messages of accountability, the teachers were motivated to find a solution rather than defend themselves. Each team knew they had the full support of their principal.

WHAT IS THE ROLE OF THE
ADMINISTRATOR AS AN EVALUATOR?

To ensure effective results in any teacher evaluation system, two factors must be considered:

1. The quality of the evaluation document and process
2. The skills of the evaluator using the system

We have observed situations where effective evaluators were able to use a rather ineffective evaluation document and/or process to assist teachers in reflecting on their performance in a way that helped them to improve. We also have seen very effective documents and/or processes rendered almost useless by ineffective evaluators. Ultimately, the skill of the evaluator is the more important factor in determining the degree of the improvement resulting from a formal evaluation.

Obviously, a well-thought-out evaluation system for both teachers and administrators puts a district in the most advantageous position for improving performance. The most effective evaluation systems collect data from multiple sources that address all aspects of a teacher's job performance. For legal reasons, it is very important to separate classroom performance activity (teaching competency) from nonteaching activity.

Some examples of classroom performance indicators are:

- The teacher informs students of the lesson objective in terms the student can easily understand.
- The teacher provides instruction that is focused on the state standards.
- The teacher frequently monitors student learning during the instruction.

Some examples of expected nonclassroom performance indicators are:

- The teacher consistently participates in professional development activities designed to enhance instructional skills.
- The teacher collaborates with others to plan and deliver effective instruction.
- The teacher adheres to the ethics of the profession.

Another critically important source of data comes from students through age-appropriate surveys. These may be conducted as a paper-and-pencil exercise or through group dialogue. In creating such a document, it is vital that the focus be on the students' personal experiences and not a rating of the teacher's performance. It is not appropriate to ask a student, "Does the teacher teach to a specified objective?" It is appropriate to ask, "Do you understand what it is that you are expected to learn?"

Historically, education as a profession has not policed itself well. Unfortunately, some evaluators have accepted mediocre or even poor performance. If we are going to meet the challenges before us, we can no longer tolerate this behavior. *No system, no matter how effective it is, can overcome the negative impact of ineffective instruction.* Ineffective practitioners must significantly improve their performance or be removed from the profession. To do anything less is condoning educational malpractice and shortchanging students who must be prepared to enter a very complicated and demanding adult world.

As the administrator prepares for the formal observation process, we believe that it is important to make expectations and feedback clear to the teacher. We suggest that the following documents be used to prepare for and conduct the observation and post-observation conference.

The principal will want to use both scheduled and unscheduled observations in the evaluation process. Scheduled evaluations will tell the evaluator if the teacher can carefully plan and teach an effective lesson. An observation without prior notice will tell the principal if the teacher plans carefully and teaches effectively on a daily basis.

The principal must be well prepared to plan and conduct an effective observation and post-observation conference. We believe that the first step should be sharing specific questions, like those in the following list, with the teacher prior to the pre-observation meeting. This helps the teacher to prepare and makes the meeting much more focused. A single form should be used by the principal to take notes during the observation and then to plan the post-observation conference. The form shown in the boxes is one that we have found to be effective. However, the principal may choose to develop a form that better fits his style and the district's evaluation process.

Preparation questions for the observation conference include:

1. What was the lesson's terminal objective?
2. Was the objective directly related to the state standards?
3. What was the task analysis for teaching the lesson?
4. How were students' past experiences used to introduce the lesson?
5. What was the sequence of the subobjectives and how were they taught?
6. What evidence was there to show that all students were engaged in the lesson?
7. What strategies were used to maintain the students' interest?
8. What strategies were used to help the students remember the lesson?
9. How was student learning monitored during the lesson?
10. How were the major components of the lesson summarized?

OBSERVATION CONFERENCE: EXAMPLES OF NOTES TAKEN DURING THE OBSERVATION

Observation Conference Example of Notes Taken during the Observation	
Ice Breaker: Her son is on the honor role. Remember to congratulate her.	Explain conference format and content: She is familiar with this format—she and I have used it several times.
Teacher Self-Analysis: Effective Instruction She has a clear objective and is teaching to the objective use factor tree to find LCD	Teacher Self-Analysis: Less Effective Instruction I wonder if she realized she didn't check to see if the students understood the objective
Neutral Transition	
Support Objective • Skill: She is monitoring • She monitored well by walking around after she taught the concept and the students were doing a practice problem • How else might she monitor • Benefit: Gives her real-time data about which students understand and which don't	
Neutral Transition	
Improvement Objective • Intro—She called only on the students who raised their hands • Needed skill: Active Participation • Needs covert activity—then overt activity • Ways to generate activity	
Neutral Transition	
Closure • Support Objective—intentionally use monitoring • Improvement Objective—generate active participation as a prerequisite to monitoring	

Observation Conference Example of a Conference with the Observed Teacher	
Ice Breaker: I see that your son made the honor roll. Please give him my congratulations.	Explain conference format and content: We are going to have a dialogue about the lesson I just observed. Please participate fully and share your thoughts with me as I share mine with you.
Teacher Self-Analysis: Effective Instruction As you reflect on the lesson, what do you think you did that was most effective in helping the students to learn the objective?	Teacher Self-Analysis: Less Effective Instruction What do you think you could have done more effectively to help the students learn the objective?

Neutral Transition: Thank you for sharing your thoughts; allow me to share some of mine.

Support Objective Do you recall when you walked among the students while they were working on the first practice problem? Tell me why you did that? Are you aware that what you did has a name? It is called <u>monitoring</u>. It is an instructional skill that makes it possible for you to know how well each student understood the instruction. If you do not monitor the students' work, you may just go on and not know which students did not understand. What other ways might you monitor student progress? I suggest you use this strategy after each subobjective and the terminal objective.

Neutral Transition: Let's look at another aspect of the lesson.

Improvement Objective As you asked questions during the lesson, did you notice that you only called on students who raised their hands? What do you think was going on in the heads of the students who did not raise their hands? If we don't call on all the students over time, we make it possible for some students to "hide." You can prevent this by employing the skill of active participation. This is a way of keeping all students involved in the lesson. What would happen if you told students to keep their hands down because you will call on someone after everyone has had time to think about an answer? Doing this requires all students to think about the question and anticipate that they may be the one called upon. Can you think of other ways of engaging all students? This is a skill that will help you to better monitor student progress. This is something I will look for as I observe future lessons. (NOTE: At this point the evaluator might want to give the teacher a copy of the Response Strategies that Ensure that All Students Are Engaged in the Learning that are included in the appendix.)

Neutral Transition: OK, now let's see if I have been an effective teacher for you. I am going to check your understanding of what we have talked about.

Closure: • We discussed a way of determining if students understand the instruction. What is the name of that skill? How will you use it in your classroom? • We also discussed a way of keeping all students involved in the lesson. Can you tell me the name of that skill? How will you use it in your classroom? What is the benefit? • As you are using both of the skill in a variety of ways, keep some notes. Periodically, I would like to check in with you and hear what your have tried and how well they have worked. I predict you are going to see some improved student learning. Keep up the good work.

WHAT IS THE ROLE OF THE ADMINISTRATOR AS A COACH?

The relatively new role of coach is evidence of a significant shift in the responsibilities of administrators from managing the school to leading the instructional practices. In the CIS, there are numerous opportunities for the administrator to act as a coach. For instance, the System encourages the administrator to take advantage of every possible opportunity to "teach the teacher" and to "learn with the teacher." These opportunities often occur in the professional development component of the faculty meeting agenda as well as during the observation/conference activities of the teacher evaluation system.

THE ADMINISTRATOR AS COACH

In a middle school in Washington State, all the teachers and the principal were learning about the importance of sharing the objective of the lesson with the students in writing and verbally, in terms they could understand. This was to ensure that students knew what they were learning and why they were learning it. The principal committed to modeling this practice in two ways. He would use the skill in all meetings and he would do demonstration lessons in the classrooms.

When he was conducting a demonstration lesson in a seventh-grade English class in character analysis, he shared the following: "Today, we are going to analyze the two main characters in our story. We are going to do that so we understand them better and so we can enjoy the story even more." Then he proceeded to teach the lesson. About three minutes into the lesson, one of the students raised his hand and, when called upon, said, "Excuse me, Mr. Jones, you did not ask us any questions to be sure we understood what you want us to do in the lesson. What if we don't know what analyze means?"

The principal responded by thanking the student and doing a quick process of making sure the students understood the objectives. He had them do a pair/share and then asked a few students some probing questions to be sure they understood that they were going to compare and contrast the traits of the two main characters to determine how they were alike and how they were different and how that played out in the story. When he was sure they had the *what* and *why* of the lesson, he proceeded to teach it.

At the end of the 20-minute lesson, he explained how he and the teachers in the school were learning to do a better job of sharing the objectives with the students. He used a metaphor. "It is like going on a trip. If you don't know where our train is going or why it is going there, you are not very likely to get on the train." He also thanked the student for the feedback that made it known that he wasn't clear about the objectives.

The student responded, "That's okay. We all learn from our mistakes and maybe our teacher can help you get better with objectives. He's pretty good at it lately."

In our work, we have discovered an interesting win-win phenomenon when a principal serves as a coach and fellow learner of new instructional strategies. The more effectively an administrator uses his time to teach and learn with his faculty members, the more satisfaction he finds in his job as leader. He is more motivated to use the skills in his own role as the teacher of teachers. This new role helps build a strong partnership between the administrator and teachers and contributes to increasing the collaborative culture of the school. The CIS provides a variety of tools to help the principal learn to fulfill this role effectively.

The story in the box demonstrates not only the power of teachers learning from and with the principal, but also the power of the principal learning from students and teachers. A key characteristic of an effective coach is someone who learns from those he coaches.

In addition to modeling lessons in the classroom, the principal-as-coach models using new skills at a faculty meeting. After a model lesson, the administrator identifies what he thinks went well and what could have been done differently to increase the effectiveness of the lesson. Teachers then offer positive "improvement" feedback. Next, the entire faculty talks as a team or in small groups about what they could do differently in their individual classrooms as a result of their experiences during the meeting. When administrators model being both a teacher and a learner, they gain the respect of the faculty and help teachers become more willing to engage in the coaching process.

Following any series of professional development activities, teachers must be held accountable for practicing and continuously improving their ability to use the newly acquired skills. In the past this has not been common practice. Teachers often attended professional development activities, participated compliantly, and then returned to their classrooms to apply only a minimal amount of what they learned.

The administrator can hold teachers accountable to apply what they have learned through either the evaluator or the coaching role. If the principal is coaching the teacher, the teacher needs to know that this is the role being employed so as to reduce the threat inherent in evaluation. If the principal is evaluating the teacher, the teacher needs to know this in order to activate the proper sense of accountability.

WHAT IS THE DIFFERENCE BETWEEN THE OBSERVATION AND CONFERENCE VERSUS EVALUATION?

It is important for administrators and teachers to understand the difference between the observation/conference coaching activities and the formal evaluation activity. They do intertwine but their separate and distinct roles must be clear. Table 11.1 compares and contrasts the two activities.

Because an administrator gathers data during a classroom observation that ultimately can be used in the formal evaluation his role in the process is complicated. There are two important questions to answer regarding this complexity:

1. Can the administrator effectively separate the observation/conference from the formal evaluation in the mind of the teacher?
2. Can the administrator eliminate the threat associated with evaluation in the mind of the teacher and maintain a focus on a collegial effort to enhance instruction?

The only honest answer to these two questions is: it depends.

Many administrators have developed very trusting relationships with faculty members, and they are able to comfortably and effectively engage teachers in a dialogue about teaching. As a result, these administrators could answer the two questions with "usually" or "most of the time." On the other hand, if an administrator is unable or unwilling to develop such relationships, the answer is: "rarely." This choice has huge ramifications on the culture of the school and how the faculty as a whole approaches the entire teaching and learning process.

Table 11.1   Observation and Conference versus Formal Evaluation

	Observation and Conference	**Formal Evaluation**
Purpose	Professional development *(Enhance performance)*	Evaluate job performance *(Employment status decision)*
Scope	Specific *(A single classroom observation)*	Broad *(All aspects of the position)*
Done by	Administrators Instructional specialists District-level supervisors External consultants	Evaluators
Accomplished with	Classroom observation notes Observation/Conference lesson plan *(No signed documents required)*	Evaluation documents *(Signed documents required)*

A MISCOMMUNICATION STORY

As we worked with districts and schools to implement the Continuous Improvement System, we have discovered a common communication problem between administrators and teachers. That problem was the lack of clarity about expectations.

One day, as Judy was working with a district-level leadership team, she heard the superintendent say, "I want every teacher in our district to work with an instructional coach at some point during the next two years." Then the superintendent moved on to the next item on the agenda. Because this was a very important expectation, Judy wondered if everyone was clear about what the superintendent was saying he wanted them to do. So she asked if everyone was clear about what the superintendent just said he expected. The answer was a resounding "yes."

Judy then asked each member of the leadership to write down what they had heard the superintendent say. Next she asked each of the eight leaders to read what they had written. Not one person had accurately heard or understood the expectation. She then invited all of them to discuss why there was lack of clarity and what the consequences might have been had it not been discovered. As a result of that conversation and some ensuing work with this leadership team, we developed the Four Phases of Change Conversation (see table 11.2).

In our experience, improvement of instruction and gains in students' academic success are much more likely to occur if the administrator skillfully fulfills the role of instructional leader. The CIS provides the administrator with a clear plan and effective process for fulfilling that role.

HOW CAN THE PRINCIPAL ENSURE SUCCESSFUL IMPLEMENTATION?

As we have worked with school personnel when they are trying to make changes in how they do their professional work, we have become aware of how important it is for the principal to be very clear about his expectations of the teachers and ensure a shared, accurate understanding of these expectations. He also needs to ensure the teachers have the resources they need to meet his expectation. We noticed that the clearer the shared understanding of and commitment to the expectations, the better the pace and quality of the implementation of a system like the CIS. The Four Phases of Change Conversation is a tool the principal can use as he builds that shared understanding of and commitment to meeting his expectations.

This tool assists the principal and teachers in the effective application of both informal and formal accountability. To facilitate this conversation successfully, the administrator must first teach it to the staff. This is followed by guided practice in the use of all four phases. Once the teachers are clear about the tool and have some idea of how to use it, the principal can use the process with any major change he is leading.

Table 11.2 details the responsibilities of the principal and the teachers during the Four Phases of Change Conversation. The first phase is devoted to stating the expectations. The second phase is a time for the principal to

Table 11.2   The Four Phases of Change Conversation

The goal of Phases One and Two is clarity.	
Phase One: Stating Expectations	
Administrator: • State expectations of the work: - What - Why - How	Teacher: • Active listening: - Bracket distractions - Suspend judgment - Listen to understand
Phase Two: Checking for Understanding	
Administrator: • Check for understanding • Ask for paraphrases	Teacher: • State understanding • Paraphrase what the leader said
The goal of Phases Three and Four is shared commitment.	
Phase Three: Soliciting Reactions	
Administrator: • Solicit reactions • Listen, paraphrase what he heard • Indicate if he is open to influence re: changes in the expectations	Teacher: • State questions and concerns • Advocate for any change that will help individuals and/or the group reach the goal
Phase Four: Determining Readiness	
Administrator: • Inquire about participants' confidence and readiness to do the work on a scale of 1 to 4, with 4 being highest • Find out what people need to be successful • Get ideas from teachers about how they should be held accountable for results and how they might hold the administrator accountable for support	Teacher: • Be honest • State needs • Generate ideas for accountability

check for understanding and clarify the expectations. The third phase allows teachers to state their reactions and concerns. The fourth phase is a time for the principal to determine which team members think they need more time in order to successfully meet the expectations.

During this conversation it is important for the principal to:

1. Clearly communicate to the person or people who must do the work what must be done, why it must be done, and how it should be done. He communicates this in writing as well as verbally.
2. Check for understanding by asking the teachers to paraphrase what they heard him say he expects. The principal corrects any misunderstandings of the expectation.
3. Solicit and address any questions or concerns teachers have about the expectation. A record of the concerns should be maintained and problem-solving groups formed to address the more complex concerns. The principal has final say about the solutions generated by these groups.
4. Check for confidence and readiness to proceed by using a scale of 1 to 4:

   1: no confidence and not at all ready
   2: minimal confidence and some readiness
   3: confident and ready
   4: very confident and very ready

Teachers record the number that best describes their readiness and confidence on a two-inch square Post-It note. They also write a brief explanation as to why they are using that number. On the back of the Post-It note, the teacher records what needs to happen for him to move up one number on the scale. It is important for the administrator to make it clear that choosing a 1 or 2 response is not a free pass to avoid what must be done. If a teacher records a 4, he notes what is needed to sustain that confidence and readiness.

This is not a quick conversation, but it is an essential one. In most cases it needs to be repeated over time as the faculty members work to meet the expectation.

Since the CIS is designed to foster the development of a culture where the continual pursuit of enhanced performance is a highly respected and valued activity, accountability is an essential component of that development. Everyone in the school must be clear about what is expected of them and be willing to do what is necessary to meet or exceed that expectation. One interesting development with the Four Phases Conversation is that, in the schools where we have taught it, some teachers have used it with their students to communicate their expectations about behavior or about major projects.

HOW CAN A SYSTEMS APPROACH TO PROFESSIONAL DEVELOPMENT HELP WITH THE IMPLEMENTATION OF THE CIS?

The System cannot be implemented successfully without effective professional development that increases content expertise as well as instructional skills. It is not possible for the principal to meet all of these professional development needs of the faculty. In addition, some school faculties are so large that it would be impossible to have all coaching come from the principal. Thus, central office personnel, specially trained staff members, and external consultants play an important role in the professional development of the teachers. These people are important sources of expertise and can help teachers improve their practice. However, they cannot hold teachers formally accountable for using what they have learned. That is still the responsibility of the building administrator. Here is an example of one program that produced effective professional development and it could be successfully used in the CIS.

When Fred served as the Assistant Superintendent of the Secondary Division for the Mesa Unified School District, he instituted the instructional specialist position. Respected teachers were selected from each campus and charged with providing ongoing professional development in their schools. These individuals were trained in such skills as essential elements of instruction, cooperative learning, mastery learning, curriculum/assessment alignment, and cognitive coaching. When the district-level supervisor of the program certified these individuals, they returned to their schools and worked closely with school-level administrators to provide effective professional development for teachers.

In the secondary division, they taught two class periods a day as they applied and refined the skills they learned in their training. They also served as demonstration classrooms in which their colleagues could observe the skillful application of instructional techniques. During the remainder of the day, they engaged in both group and individual teacher professional development activities. It is important to clarify that the instructional specialists played absolutely no role in the teacher evaluation process. To do so would have undermined the coaching relationship they needed to develop with the teachers.

Even though this program was initiated at the secondary level, it is equally applicable in the elementary school. At the elementary level, the program can be implemented through either one person in a full-time position or two people sharing a position. In a shared position, both teachers can work in a single classroom. One teacher is assigned to teach in the morning with one curricular focus. The other takes the class in the afternoon and focuses on a different area in the curriculum. When the teachers are teaching, their classrooms serve as demonstration sites; when they are not teaching, they provide professional development for individuals or groups of teachers.

The use of on-staff instructional coaches sends the message that high-quality instruction is a priority. Utilizing these coaches greatly impacts the informal accountability in the school culture. When teachers see their colleagues demonstrating improved instructional techniques, they are more motivated to try the new techniques with their own students. Because their colleague/coach does not act as supervisor or evaluator, the teachers are more likely to take the risk of trying the new ideas with their students and willingly accept coaching feedback. As more and more teachers gain the confidence necessary to commit to continuously improving their practice, the culture increasingly becomes one based on effective informal accountability. As this cycle of continuous improvement continues, there is a professional confidence that develops. As a result, teachers learn to view the administrator as a leader who is also continuously learning about instruction, modeling these new skills in classrooms and meetings. They also become more comfortable when the administrator is working with them in the role of formal evaluator.

This instructional specialist program proved to be a forerunner of similar programs occurring in districts across the country. If your school or district decides to implement the CIS, this model could be very helpful. The instructional coaches would all be trained in the components of the CIS and could help the principal lead the implementation process. If your school or district does not currently have a teacher-as-coach program, we strongly encourage you to explore the possibility. Our experience indicates that this is time and money well spent.

Obviously, the optimal condition is for every member of a school to be personally responsible for the quality and impact of his performance. However, this is not a behavior that all people readily exhibit. Being personally responsible requires that a person:

1. Welcomes feedback about the quality and impact of his performance and learns from this feedback.
2. Takes a positive collaborative approach rather than a reactive one in interactions with other members of the team.
3. Is open to learning from his mistakes rather than making excuses for them or blaming them on someone else.

Therefore, a key element in creating this optimal condition is for the principal to take great care in hiring faculty members. Our best advice is to hire people for their talent and the quality of their character and not for their years of experience or the degrees they hold. The high-quality person will learn the job, and you, as the administrator, will have far fewer accountability concerns.

Chapter Twelve

Checking Progress

HOW WILL YOU KNOW IF YOU ARE
EFFECTIVELY IMPLEMENTING THE CIS?

During the process of implementing the CIS principals and teachers frequently ask, "How are we doing? Are we there yet?" One way to begin to explore the answers to these questions is to complete the Continuous Improvement System Assessment Form shown in table 12.1.

Initially, the leadership team meets to complete the form and individual team members rate each component on the form. Then they share their individual ratings and engage in a dialogue about their rationale for their ratings. After each member has spoken, the team continues the dialogue until they reach consensus on a rating for each item. When the leadership team reaches consensus on all the items, the process is repeated with the entire faculty.

Typically, the ratings from the two groups are divergent and this leads to a rich dialogue concerning how successfully the CIS is being implemented. This dialogue produces clear plans that stipulate next steps for the leadership team and for the staff as a whole, because their ratings show where they are successful and where they need to focus next. Because everyone has had the opportunity to shape this plan, there is usually strong support and the next steps are quickly taken.

This form can be used at various times during the school year to monitor progress in the implementation and utilization of the CIS. However, it should always be used at the end of the school year as a planning tool for the next school year. This allows administrators and teachers to benefit from a full year of their successes and their mistakes, allowing them to learn from both.

Table 12.1 Continuous Improvement System Assessment Form

Assessment → Component ↓	Still in the Starting Blocks	Gaining Momentum	In Full Stride	Hitting the Finish Line	Comments: What are the positive factors and/or the inhibitors?
			BE HONEST!		
School Vision					
Academic Mission					
Core Commitments					
Meeting Norms					
School Rules					
Instructional Calendars					
Effective Instruction					
Common Assessments					
Data Charts					
Data and Dialogue					
Meeting Room					
Instructional Teams					
Reteach/ Retest					
Faculty Meeting					
Professional Development					
Leadership Team					
Four Phases of Change Conv.					
Overall Rating					

Once each component is rated, careful attention should be given to the last column on the right side of the form. It is important to identify the factors that are successfully moving the component toward the finish line, as well as those factors that are inhibiting progress. With this information in hand, the leadership team is in a good position to make plans for the future. The optimal approach is to select two to three successful factors to be reinforced and two to three inhibiting factors that must be addressed. Focusing on more dilutes the effectiveness of the effort.

Note the direction at the top of the form that reads BE HONEST! In *Good to Great* (2001), Jim Collins identified two distinctive attributes of the highly successful companies in the study. He reported, "These companies infused the entire reformation process with the brutal facts. They then developed a simple, yet deeply insightful, frame of reference for all decisions based on these facts."

Because there is a natural tendency for most people to inflate their responses, it is important to require clear evidence for any rating. Inflated ratings may allow people to feel good for a very short time but ultimately they are detrimental to long-term success.

The form was intentionally created with an even number of response options. This format forces people to make a real decision about the level of implementation as opposed to selecting the safe middle column.

CRITICAL QUESTION EXAMPLES

The following questions may be used to generate the dialogue required to thoughtfully complete the form. These are only examples and we encourage principals and leadership teams to customize the list so it fits their needs.

School Vision

1. Did each faculty member have the opportunity to participate in the writing of the document?
2. Is the document professional in appearance and displayed in all the appropriate locations in the school?
3. Is the statement discussed frequently during faculty meetings?

Academic Mission

1. Is the bar set at a realistic and attainable level that stretches but does not break both the faculty members and the students?
2. Do both faculty and students know and pursue the academic mission?

3. Is the document professional in appearance and displayed in all the appropriate locations in the school?

Core Commitments

1. Did each faculty member have the opportunity to participate in the writing of the core commitments?
2. Is the document professional in appearance and displayed in all the appropriate locations in the school?
3. Are the statements discussed frequently during faculty meetings?
4. Are the statements "lived" by all educators? Are they evident in the daily interactions among teachers and with students?

Meeting Norms

1. Did each faculty member have the opportunity to participate in the writing of the norms?
2. Do the norms appear on all meeting agendas?
3. Are the norms observed during all meetings?

School Rules

1. Are the rules set forth in a document that is professional in appearance and displayed in all the appropriate locations in the school?
2. Are the rules written in such a way that they are positive targets rather than threats?
3. Are the rules discussed frequently among the teachers and with students?
4. Are specific behaviors taught in support of the rules?

Instructional Calendars

1. Are the calendars professional in appearance and displayed in all the appropriate locations in the school?
2. Are the calendars developed using the state standards?
3. Do the calendars contain both new and review content?
4. Does the principal monitor the calendars monthly?

Effective Instruction

1. Are a variety of research-based instructional strategies effectively being used by all teachers?
2. Are students fully engaged in the learning?
3. Are students achieving the academic mission?
4. Is there an effective reteach/retest system in place?

Common Assessments

1. Are the assessments developed at the same time as the instructional calendar?
2. Are items on the assessment correctly grouped and linked to the state standards?
3. Does the language and rigor on the assessment match that used in the state standards performance objective?

Data Charts

1. Are the classroom and grade-level/subject charts presented in a professional manner and displayed in appropriate locations?
2. Are the classroom and grade-level/subject charts effectively used by the instructional teams and the leadership team?
3. Is there a clear trail that tracks any given performance objective from the instructional calendar to the assessment to the data chart?
4. Do students understand the charts and use them to monitor their own progress?

Data–Dialogue

1. Is the facilitator skilled in leading these dialogues?
2. Do teachers authentically and skillfully participate in these dialogues?
3. Do these dialogues result in clarity about expectations and a commitment to meeting these expectations?

Meeting Room

1. Are all data and materials readily available in the room?
2. Do teachers have access to computers, printers, and the Internet in the meeting room?
3. Does the room communicate that it is a place of business?

Instructional Teams

1. Do the teams meet on a regular basis?
2. Do the teams function in a collegial, collaborative, and productive manner?
3. Do teams have evidence of higher levels of student learning?
4. Does data drive the work of the teams?

Reteach/Retest

1. Is there a systemic approach to the reteach/retest process in place and do all faculty members understand and successfully apply the process?

2. Do students who did not meet the academic mission and students who did meet the academic mission both participate in the program?
3. Are new instructional strategies used?
4. Is there clear evidence that the process has a positive impact on student achievement?

Faculty Meeting

1. Are the school vision, academic mission, core commitments, and school rules included as regular agenda items?
2. Does the faculty as a whole engage in the processes of data analysis and sharing of instructional strategies?
3. Does the agenda contain targeted professional development designed to help teachers learn the skills necessary to address an identified student learning problem?

Professional Development

1. Is the content of the professional development internally identified?
2. Is the training and implementation support provided over a sufficient period of time to ensure that new skills are effectively acquired?
3. Are people held accountable to effectively use the skills following the training?

Leadership Team

1. Does the team meet on a regular basis?
2. Does the team function in a collegial, collaborative, and productive manner?
3. Does data drive the work of the team?

Four Phases of Change Conversation

1. Do leaders clearly state expectations?
2. Do leaders check faculty members' understanding of the expectations?
3. Does the leader provide the support that helps faculty members meet the expectations, while holding them accountable?

We work from the assumption that the success of any organization is primarily determined by two factors: (1) the effectiveness and efficiency of the system that is in place, and (2) the quality of the individual and collective performance demonstrated by the people in the organization. This leads us to continually ask two salient questions:

1. What is the next step in making the CIS more effective and efficient?
2. How can the levels of the individual and collective performance be raised?

The Continuous Improvement System Assessment Form initiates a dialogue that will help to answer these questions. The assessment is designed to send the message that the status quo is definitely unacceptable. If continuous improvement is to be realized, the administrators and faculty members must continuously explore ways to raise their individual and collective performance level. When effort is consistently given, we have seen schools move from underperforming to successful and from successful to excelling.

As a final thought about "How are we doing and are we there yet?" we remind you that the CIS is designed to impact the culture of the school. A culture cannot be "taught." It must be experienced, demonstrated, and nurtured through exemplary behavior. It must be lived as faculty members work to address sustained demands for excellence and as they welcome the monitoring of their progress in meeting these demands. As the culture changes, teacher efficacy grows and students achieve at higher levels. Once you have clear evidence that the culture of the school, teacher efficacy, and student achievement are being positively impacted, you can say that the school is on its way toward being in full stride.

A CHANGE STORY

It was near the end of the 2007-2008 school year when the principal and Fred Skoglund were meeting with the school's leadership team. The principal and the faculty had spent the year working diligently to implement the CIS and it was time to use the Continuous Improvement System Assessment Form to analyze the level of implementation. As Fred initiated the assessment exercise, he asked, "As you think back over this year, what has changed?"

One of the leadership team members immediately replied, "Everything! We have to face real-time data. Now we talk to each other. We talk about what kids are learning and how we can be more effective at teaching them and not about all the reasons they can't learn."

The principal is now implementing the System in her third school. She states, "After my experiences in two prior schools, I can't imagine working in a school that does not have this system in place."

Conclusion

In closing, we ask you to again consider a question that appears on the instructional team meeting agenda: Who are the students who did not meet the academic mission, and what will we do to address their needs?

As we work together as educators to genuinely embrace the "learning for all" vision, this may be the most important question we must answer. Finding an answer to this critical question is a time-consuming and messy process because there is no single solution that will work in every school. Meeting the needs of all students in a school requires a fundamental change in how that school operates. Each school is a unique entity and so all faculty members must clarify their vision and pursue it vigorously by taking the actions that best fit their particular situation.

Dr. Larry Lezotte is frequently quoted as saying, "Educators are doing the best they know how to do given the context in which they find themselves." This statement is both provocative and profound. It challenges us as educators to face the critical issues of acquiring new knowledge and changing the context in which that knowledge will be applied.

The collaborative work of the instructional teams, the leadership team, and the faculty of the school is the core of the CIS. These teams focus on the identifying the issues surrounding teaching and learning in the school and problem solving how to most effectively address those issues. In this process, administrators and teachers share their current knowledge and explore ways to more effectively apply what they already know. They also identify the need for new ideas and procedures necessary to address the specific issues present in the school. When these needs are identified and owned by the faculty, the professional development component of the CIS assists educators to procure the information and training that will help them to acquire new knowledge.

The Continuous Improvement System changes the context in which educators find themselves. The CIS requires faculty members to set a lofty but reasonable expectation for student achievement and make commitments as to how they will conduct themselves in the pursuit of an academic mission. It requires teachers to collaborate in selecting critical curriculum and creating common assessment tools that provide real-time student achievement data. The CIS makes the student achievement data public and calls for that data to be used in ways that actually drive instruction. It changes teaching from work done in isolation to work accomplished collectively. It makes true partners of administrators and teachers.

Many of the individual components of the Continuous Improvement System are not new concepts. What is new is that in the CIS, the proven individual components are combined into a comprehensive system that positively impacts the day-to-day effectiveness of a school. As administrators and teachers gain a clear understanding of the interrelatedness of these proven concepts, they benefit by using them as a problem-solving system, not stand-alone solutions. The result is systemic and long-lasting improvement.

We have seen the Continuous Improvement System make a very significant difference for teachers and students in multiple schools. We invite you to use the System to help you identify and address the curriculum and instructional practice issues impacting your school. When implemented with fidelity, we can say with confidence that the CIS will make a positive difference in teacher performance and student achievement in your school too.

References

Coleman, James "Equality of Educational Opportunity," U.S. Office of Education, 1966.

Collins, Jim. 2001. *Good to Great.* New York: HarperCollins Publishing.

Edmonds, R. and Frederiksen, J. R. *Search for Effective Schools: the Identification and Analysis of City Schools That Are Instructionally Effective for Poor Children*, Cambridge, Mass.: Harvard University Center for Urban Studies, 1978.

Education Week, June 2010, volume 36, issue 29.

Glasser, William. 1990. The Quality School. *Phi Delta Kappan* 71 (6): 424–35.

Halper, Jan. 1989. *Quiet Desperation: The Truth About Successful Men.* New York: Warner Books.

Herzberg, Frederick. 1993. *The Motivation to Work.* London: Transaction Publishers.

Hunter, Madeline, *Mastery Teaching*, El Segundo, Ca.: TIP Publications, 1982.

Joyce, Bruce, and Beverly Showers. 1988. *Student Achievement through Staff Development.* New York: Longman.

Lezotte, Lawrence W. 1997. *Learning for All.* Okemos, MI: Effective Schools Products.

Marzano, Robert. 2002. *Designing and Teaching Learning Goals and Objectives Strategies.* Alexandria, VA: ASCD.

Marzano, Robert. 2003. *What Works in Schools.* Alexandria, VA: ASCD.

Marzano, Robert, Tim Waters, and Brian McNulty. 2005. *School Leadership That Works.* Alexandria, VA: ASCD.

Miller, Kirsten. 2003. *School, Teacher and Leadership Impacts on Student Achievement* [policy brief]. Aurora, CO: Mid-continent Research for Education and Learning.

Senge, Peter. 1990. *The Fifth Discipline.* New York: Doubleday.

Taylor, B. M., M. P. Pressley, and P. D. Pearson. 2002. Effective Schools and Accomplished Teachers. *Elementary School Journal* 101 (2): 121–66.

Waters, J. T., Marzano, R. J., and McNulty, B. A., "Balanced Leadership: What 30 Years of Research Tells Us About the Effects of Leadership on Student Achievement," Aurora, Co.: Mid-Continent Research for Education and Learning, 2003.

Suggested Readings

Christensen, Clayton. *Disrupting Class: How Disruptive Innovation Will Change the Way the World Learns.* New York: McGraw-Hill, 2008.

DuFour, Richard, Rebecca DuFour, Robert Eaker, and Gayle Karhanek. *Whatever It Takes: How Professional Learning Communities Respond When Kids Don't Learn.* Bloomington, IN: Solution Tree, 2004.

Eaker, Robert, Richard DuFour, and Rebecca DuFour. *Getting Started : Reculturing Schools to Become Professional Learning Communities.* Bloomington, IN: Solution Tree, 2002.

Glasser, William. *Choice Theory.* New York: HarperCollins, 1998.

Glasser, William. *Choice Theory in the Classroom.* New York: Harper, 1998.

Guskey, Thomas. *Implementing Mastery Learning.* Wadsworth Publishing, 1996.

Hall, Gene, and Shirley Hord. *Implementing Change: Patterns, Principles and Potholes.* Boston: Pearson Education, 2006.

Hall, Gene, and Shirley Hord. *Taking Charge of Change.* Alexandria, VA: ASCD, 1987.

Hall, Pete, and Alisa Simeral. *Building Teachers' Capacity for Success.* Alexandria, VA: ASCD, 2008.

Kohn, Alfie. *Punished by Rewards.* Boston: Houghton Mifflin, 1993.

Lezotte, Lawrence. *Creating the Total Quality Effective School.* Okemos, MI: Effective Schools Products, 1992.

Lezotte, Lawrence. *The Effective School Process: A Proven Path to Learning for All.* Okemos, MI: Effective Schools Products, 1997.

Lezotte, Lawrence. *Learning for All.* Okemos, MI: Effective Schools Products, 1997.

Lezotte, Lawrence, and Kathleen McKee. *Assembly Required: A Continuous School Improvement System.* Okemos, MI: Effective Schools Products, 2002.

Marzano, Robert. *What Works in Schools.* Alexandria, VA: ASCD, 2003.

Marzano, Robert, Debra Pickering, and Jane Pollock. *Classroom Instruction That Works.* Alexandria, VA: ASCD, 2001.

Marzano, Robert, Timothy Waters, and Brian McNulty. *School Leadership That Works.* Alexandria, VA: ASCD, 2005.

Popham, W. James. *Classroom Assessment: What Teachers Should Know.* Needham Heights, MA: Allyn and Bacon, 1995.

Popham, W. James. *Transformative Assessment.* Alexandria, VA: ASCD, 2008.

Senge, Peter. *Schools That Learn.* New York: Doubleday Publishing, 2000.

Sergiovanni, Thomas. 1984. Leadership and Excellence in Schooling. *Educational Leadership* 4 (5): 14–23.

Weinstein, Carol. 1991. Expectations and High School Change: Teacher-Researcher Collaboration to Prevent School Failure. *American Journal of Community Psychology* 19 (3): 333–63.

Wigfield, Allan, Jacquelyn Eccles, and Daniel Rodriguez. 1998. The Development of Children's Motivation in School Context. *Review of Research in Education* 23: 73–118.

Appendix

COMMUNICATION

The Assumption Sort and Inventory

The following steps guide team members through a process of naming their assumptions about a change and identifying those that actually are true and could be impediments to reaching the desired result of a change process. The team members sort and cluster their assumptions into groups. Then people with factual information that affirms or counters these identified assumptions share what they know with the group. These people with the factual information could be teachers, the principal, district office administrators, or even the superintendent. Once the team is clear on which assumptions are true and which are false, their dialogue can become much more productive because they will not be wasting time worrying about things they think to be true. They can problem solve the issues that are true and can impede progress toward a targeted change.

1. Split the participants into table groups and assign someone to record the proceedings.
2. Ask people to define the word *assumption*.
3. Share the dictionary definition: *An assumption is something taken for granted.*
4. Ask them to think about the assumptions they have on a particular aspect of the work being done by the team. (This process can also be used with work that they know is coming in the near future.)
5. Share an example of an assumption about the work.
6. Ask everyone to write down three to five assumptions they have, one per Post-It note.

7. Ask one table to post their assumptions on a flip chart page and to name each category for the rest of the groups.
8. Ask the rest of the groups to cluster their Post-It notes with the first group's offering if they have the same/similar assumptions, or create a new category.
9. Repeat this process with every group until all assumptions are posted in clusters of like assumptions.
10. Invite the individual or individuals who can clarify which assumptions are correct and which are not to share this information with the full team.

If there are numerous assumptions, the facilitator should address the assumptions that were mentioned by the greatest number of groups first. If the team hears about too many assumptions in one sitting, they are likely to fall victim to auditory fatigue.

Usually, the "act of good will" of addressing the first set of assumptions is sufficient. However, if significant resistance to the change remains, a second meeting should be held to continue to address the ongoing assumptions.

Differentiating between Thoughts and Feelings

One of the critical skills for members of any team is effective communication. This skill set has many components and one of the most important is to be able to know when a person is sending or receiving a message that is a thought versus a feeling. This is important because a thought can be evaluated and found correct or incorrect. A feeling cannot. Feelings are not right or wrong; they just are. The following process helps people differentiate between the two.

Naming Our Thoughts and Feelings

1. The principal clearly states that everyone's thoughts *and* everyone's feelings matter as they work together to implement the system (or whatever change is their current focus).
2. He explains that periodically someone will facilitate a checking in of both types of information—facts and feelings.
3. He teaches the following two sentence stems that can be applied to any topic:

Speaking from the head about _____. I think _____ because _____.

Speaking from the heart about _____.

I am _____ because _____.

4. He explains that feelings are not right or wrong; they just are. He also clarifies that emotions create energy and that is why he wants the team members to become skilled in identifying and sharing their feelings when appropriate.

5. Next, he explains that in the "heart" statement, the speaker must use one feeling word to fill in the blank after "I am___." It is helpful if faculty members understand why the statement contains the verb *am* rather than *feel*. If the statement used the verb *feel* instead of *am* there is a strong tendency to slip back to a head type of communication. People typically say something like, "I feel that this is a good first step." This statement may be accurate on a factual level, but it does not tell the listener what the speaker is feeling. The verb *am* ensures that the speaker will state a feeling. Some people are less comfortable speaking from the heart than others. Consequently, we have included a list of feeling words in table A.1 to help team members develop a feeling vocabulary.

6. The principal shares his thoughts and feelings about the topic of discussion by completing the sentence stems. If this were applied to writing a school vision, an example of his head statement might be: "I think we have written a very powerful vision statement because it is clear, short, and easy to remember. My evidence is that I have asked ten people today what it is and what it means to them, and they all could repeat the statement. All of them said it expressed something about all of us working together to ensure all students learn at their highest levels." An example of his heart statement might be: "I am encouraged because that was not true about our previous vision statement."

7. He asks each team member to complete the two sentence stems in writing about the topic of discussion.

8. He facilitates sharing the statements. The sharing process will vary depending on the size of the group. Some possible ways include:

- Each team member posts his written stems on chart paper. This can be done randomly or by clustering like items together. The paper is placed in the faculty room so staff members can read what their colleagues wrote.
- Team members share their responses in small groups.
- Team members volunteer to share their responses.
- They turn their responses in to the principal. He reads them and then shares them with his building leadership team.

Sharing thoughts and feelings in a focused and intentional way can help prevent and solve the inevitable problems that occur when implementing any change because change is both a mental and an emotional process. This is definitely the case when implementing the CIS. Skillfully sharing and hearing *both* thoughts and feelings during a dialogue helps team members know what it's like to be in the shoes of a colleague. Usually people find it easier to share their thoughts than their feelings.

However, change stirs emotions and when you implement the Continuous Improvement System you create change. Those emotions may be mild or intense, but they are part of the change process, and they can result in resistance. Consequently, it is important that team members become skilled in accurately sharing and respecting each other's feelings in order to prevent that resistance. The table that follows is helpful in building that skill.

Table A.1   The Three As of Sharing and Hearing Feelings

ACKNOWLEDGE . . . Team members name their feelings. They can choose one of the following feeling words if they are having difficulty naming it.			
Mild Expressions of Emotion			
Mad	Glad	Sad	Scared
annoyed	pleased	down	uneasy
bothered	amused	blue	tense
peeved	content	resigned	concerned
irritated	comfortable	disappointed	anxious
miffed	relieved	hurt	nervous
Moderate Expressions of Emotion			
disgusted	cheerful	discouraged	alarmed
harassed	delighted	drained	worried
resentful	hopeful	unhappy	vulnerable
upset	eager	distressed	frightened
angry	happy	burdened	overwhelmed
Intense Expression of Emotion			
enraged	enthralled	miserable	petrified
incensed	elated	crushed	terrified
furious	excited	humiliated	horrified
livid	ecstatic	despondent	full of dread
irate	exuberant	anguished	frantic
ACCEPT . . . They own their individual feelings, knowing it is not bad to have the feeling but it is harmful to propel ourselves into a reactive position and/or resistance behavior.			
APPROPRIATELY SHARE . . . They individually articulate their individual feelings. I am . . . The person states the feeling because . . . and say why he is experiencing this particular emotion.			

A Case Study Protocol—Framing the Problem for Possible Solutions

1. Name the Problem (*5 min.*)
Share your problem using the two framing sentence stems:

   - My problem is . . .
   - I consider it a problem because . . .

2. Check for Understanding (*5 min.*)
Invite one person from the table team to share his understanding of your problem.
3. Describe Targeted Results (*5 min.*)
Talk about the results you would like to see as result of an effective solution to the problem.
4. Check for Understanding (*5 min.*)
Ask a person from the table to share his understanding of your targeted results.
5. Generate Possible Solutions (*20 min.*)

   - *Round One (10 min.)*

     Each person suggests a possible solution. A facilitator records these ideas on a flip chart page. In this first round of possible solutions, each person suggests a different solution.

   - *Round Two (10 min.)*

     Each person suggests a second possible solution and again the DIF records the ideas. In this round of possible solutions, people can extend or deepen ideas generated in the first round. They can do this with the solution they suggested or with another person's suggested solution. They can combine solutions.

   - During both of these rounds, the facilitator is listening, not participating. He may ask questions for clarification of any of the solutions.

6. Summarize the Impact of the Protocol (*10 min.*)
Use the following sentence stems to summarize the impact of the mini–case study on you.

   - Right now I think . . . about the problem I presented.
   - Possible take-aways for me are . . .
   - My next step is . . .

Total Time for Each Presenter of a Problem: 45 minutes

A GLOSSARY OF INSTRUCTIONAL STRATEGIES

Models of instruction usually include a collection of strategies a teacher can use in the classroom. This glossary describes strategies that are parts of some major models of instruction developed over the past 25 years.

Direct Instruction

8/2 to 2 Rule: When giving a lecture, a teacher never talks longer than 8 minutes without taking a 2-second to 2-minute break during which he guides the students in the use of a strategy for processing what he has been saying.

Move Away from Speaker: One of the most common ways that a teacher teaches is to share information verbally and ask questions of the students. When a teacher uses this strategy it is important that the teacher move away from that student who is speaking. This includes more learners in the dialogue. The teacher should not turn his back on the speaking student, but should back up or move sideways as surreptitiously as possible. If the teacher does not do this, the dialogue becomes a conversation between the teacher and the student answering the question and as a result many of the students lose interest in the exchange.

Silent Sage: The teacher gives directions or shares content-level information by writing on the overhead, or using a PowerPoint or a SMART Board. The entire set of directions is given and the content is explained in writing and the students read along. No words are spoken. At the end of the writing, which becomes known as "sage-ing," the teacher facilitates a discussion of what the students learned while the teacher was using this strategy.

Sponge Activities: The teacher organizes short, meaningful activities that "sponge up" time that would otherwise be wasted during the beginning of the class or during transitions from one activity to another activity during class time. These activities are relevant to the content the students are studying.

Cooperative Learning

A/B Check: The teacher asks students to pair up, and designates one student as A and the other student as B. This allows the teacher to give quick and efficient directions such as "A answer questions 1 and 2, B answer 3 and 4, and then share with one another." A can quiz B and vice-versa.

Birthday Line: Students form a line in the order of their birthdays via hand signals. Then they number off to form cooperative learning groups.

Chart Exchange: The teacher forms groups and assigns numbers to them. He assigns one topic of the content being studied to the odd-numbered tables and a different topic to the even-numbered tables. Groups follow the teacher's directions and record their work on a flip chart page. At the signal they exchange charts and examine the other group's work, comparing and/or contrasting it to their own. The comparison can be a general one or it can be based on specific directions. This works particularly well when the focus of the study for the group contains concepts that are different but related.

Climate Intervention: Students are placed in teams, and each team is assigned a time during the school year or semester. At its assigned time the team changes the climate of the room. The change (intervention) can follow a theme if the team wishes. The team can use posters, plants, student work, garlands, music, and so on.

Collaborative Quiz: Students work in pairs, trios, or quartets to answer the questions on a quiz. The teacher points out that quizzes are to find out what they don't know so they can find the information.

Expert Group Development: This is a version of a cooperative learning jigsaw. A group of students learns a concept and decides how they are going to share it. This group is the expert group. They then share this information with another group of students. This is the learning group. The expert group reconvenes and critiques how the teaching went and what they learned from the other representatives of the other expert groups. Any resource on cooperative learning will have more detailed directions on this strategy. It is one of the most complex of the cooperative learning strategies and should be used with more mature learning groups and only after the students in this group have practiced worked in cooperative groups for a considerable amount of time.

Floating Chart: Students work in small groups and record their work on a large sheet of newsprint or on a flip chart page. Each group can work on a different concept or piece of the content or they can work on the same piece or concept. When they have recorded their work, the charts are then "floated" or moved to another group. Each small group processes the information from the previous group. The floating sequence is continued until the groups receive their own chart back or all information has been processed. It is important to change the focus of the processing each time the small group receives a new chart. The following is a list of ways to make those changes. Ask the small groups to:

- Mark the best ideas on their neighbors' chart
- Mark the most challenging idea
- Add an idea or an item of information that they have not seen on any chart
- Mark ideas or information that require higher-level thinking
- Make one suggestion for improving the information or ideas on the chart
- Mark any places that are unclear with a question mark
- Draw a symbol or an icon that represents the information on the page

Add other ideas for processing the information as needed or as dictated by the age and experience of the students. It is important to limit the maximum number of times for floating the chart to six and the minimum number of times to three. Provide a variety of colored marking pens to add visual interest to the charts.

Floating Test: Students are put in groups of two, three, or four. Each group answers a test question. The answers are "floated" to another group and the second group corrects the answer. This process can be repeated with new questions. A derivation is to have the new group add to the answer and have a third group check the answer.

Forming Groups: It is important to have a variety of strategies for forming small groups in the classroom. Try numbering off, using clothes color, birthdays, or playing cards. It is recommended that the grouping be done nonverbally when possible to keep noise and confusion to a minimum.

Inside/Outside Circle: Students form two circles, one within the other. They face each other. On signal, students share information on a given topic. Inner circle rotates and the process is repeated based on what the teacher wants them to share with one another. Another option is to have the students express to their partner what they want to know about a topic they are going to be studying. Still another option is to have the students periodically share with one another what they have learned about a topic. The power of this strategy is the mini-dialogue between the students as the circles rotate. The weakness of this strategy is that the teacher does not hear what the students were saying. One way to address this weakness is to have full class discussion of what students shared in the circles.

Jigsaw: Information the students are to learn is broken into "chunks" and each chunk is assigned to one student in a small group. The students study their chunks and then teach them to the others in their small group.

Quiz Exchange: The teacher gives a quiz in the traditional manner with students writing their answers. Students then pair up, and after comparing answers they make any changes or additions they think necessary in their own answers. At this point the quizzes can be collected by the teacher and graded. Another option is to have the students exchange papers again and correct each other's papers. The teacher emphasizes that the most important purpose of a quiz is to point out what we do not know so we can do what is necessary to learn that information.

Round Robin: In a small group, one student begins sharing and then the person next to him shares. This continues around the group until everyone has had a turn. The rounds can be repeated as often as necessary. The groups should be no larger than six students and the items they share can be answers, questions, ideas, suggestions, and so forth.

Talking Chips: While working in small groups, students are given a certain number of chips. They are to put a chip in the center of the table each time they talk. Each student should use all of his chips, and no student can talk anymore when his chips are gone.

Think/Pair/Share: Pair up the students. All students are asked to think of a concept, to answer a question in their mind, or to solve a problem at a higher thinking level. Next, they pair up and share their answers. They are asked to combine the best of both answers and then the answers are shared at a whole-class level.

Think/Pair/Square: Students pair up with a partner. They are asked to think of a concept, to answer a question in their mind, or to solve a problem mentally. Students pair up and compare their thoughts, answers, or solutions, adjusting the results so they use the best thinking of each individual. Then two pairs combine by *squaring up* to compare the concept, answer, or solution from each of the two pairs. Again, they synthesize the results to produce the best possible thinking of all four students. The concept, answer, or solution of each quartet is shared with the whole class.

Walk 'n' Talk: Students pair up and walk in a designated area while they read and discuss an assigned topic. They are given a specific time limit and a specific task to complete relative to the information they are reading. It may be a question to answer, a summary sentence to write, or a picture to draw. When they return to their desks the teacher facilitates a process for reporting what they learned.

Active Participation for All Students

Covert/Overt: The teacher clarifies that students will always have time to think before they have to speak to answer a question. The students learn that the teacher will always ask the question at the covert level first in order to provide this time for thinking. This is the undercover level. The teacher asks the question of the whole class first, while all the students are thinking what the answer may be. Their thinking is covert or "undercover." Then the teacher takes the question to the overt level, the "out in the open" level.

ROM (Response Opportunity Minimum):   The teacher explains that he wants to be sure that all students have an equitable opportunity to "show what they know." To do so, he facilitates the students setting a *guaranteed* minimum number of times they will be called upon during a week at the secondary level or during a day at the elementary level. Both teachers and individual students develop strategies for tracking the response opportunities. The purpose of this is twofold. One is that all students realize that responding to questions is a desirable thing, not a punishment. The other is that there is a strong tendency to call on 20 percent of the students 80 percent of the time and this strategy ensures a more equitable distribution.

Response Strategies that Ensure that All Students Are Engaged in the Learning   Since the question-and-answer process is one of the key ways teachers and students converse about content, it is critically important that *all* students are consistently and equitably invited into this question-and-answer exchange. Thus, it is essential to have a variety of techniques for inviting students to show what they know. A starting list of those strategies includes:

- Teacher asks the question and chooses the student to answer the question, taking care to ask all students an equitable number of questions over time.

- Teacher gives the answer and the students ask the question. This is a jeopardy technique.
- The teacher asks the question and calls on pairs of students.
- Teacher records questions on the overhead, students record the answers individually. The teacher records his answer and students compare their answers and make any necessary corrections. These steps are done without talking. A variation is to invite students to exchange their papers and make additional corrections before the teacher shares the answer. It is important to have students challenge the answers of the teacher if they disagree. There will be some times when the student's answer may be more correct than the teacher's and the teacher needs to acknowledge having learned from the student. Sometimes a student's answer is as equally correct as the teacher's. At this point it is important to note that many questions have more than one answer. Finally, if a student challenges the answer, but their answer is clearly wrong, it is critical to honor the dignity of that student. The teacher should ask how the student arrived at that answer. The teacher can then praise the thinking process but point out the error in the conclusion. It is essential that students understand that mistakes help us learn.
- Teacher asks a question and a student is called upon to answer. After the answer from the student and feedback from the teacher as to correctness of the answer, the student asks a question. Another student is called upon to answer. This process is repeated no more than five times.
- Teacher asks a question and tosses a ball to a student to designate who is to answer the question. After answering the question, the student identifies another student and tosses the ball to him. Once the ball is caught, the teacher asks a question of that student. The advantage of this strategy is that the teacher can customize the questions to ensure student success. The disadvantage of this strategy is that the student who is to answer is identified in advance and that student's level of concern is at its peak. The rest of the class may be at an intellectual recess because they know they do not need to answer the question. One way to address this disadvantage is the teacher makes it clear that the next student to get the ball will be asked to build on the answer of the previous students. The building process should be used periodically and should be repeated for only two rounds. The teacher does not want to repeat it more than twice, or students will shorten and weaken their responses because they know the teacher always asks for more.
- Students write their names on two to five file cards. The cards are thoroughly shuffled and then the teacher asks a question, waits three seconds, and calls on the student whose name is on the file card on top of the deck. This strategy ensures that, over time, every student will be called on two

to three times, depending on the number of cards labeled with student names.

- The teacher asks students to write their names on three Popsicle sticks. He puts these sticks in a cup and pulls sticks from the cup to determine who will answer a question after he has asked it at the covert level. This means he asks, "How does the legislature differ from the executive branch of our government? Think of two or three ways." Then, he pulls sticks from the cup and calls on the students whose names appear.

Tracking Responses: It is important to keep track of who has had the opportunity to respond to a question or to demonstrate knowledge in some way. With all tracking strategies, it is important for the teacher to explain to the students that you are trying to ensure they receive equal opportunity to show what they know and to demonstrate what they can do. Specific tracking strategies include:

- Mark an x or a check mark by the name of students on the seating chart or class roster when that student has been asked a question.
- Ask students to record their names on two to five index cards. Shuffle the cards and use them to determine who will answer the question. After you have used all of the cards, reshuffle and use the deck again. The students can also record some personal information about themselves such as their favorite food, sport, or place they want to travel on the card. This helps the teacher learn additional information about the students.
- Write the names of students (or have them write them themselves) on Popsicle sticks and place the sticks in a container. Draw them out one at a time and call on the student whose name is on the stick. After all of the sticks have been drawn, put all the sticks back in the container and use the sticks again.
- Ask students to keep track of how many times they have been called on and to give that data to you. This can be on a slip of paper, a Post-It Note on their desktop, a student notebook, or a journal.
- Use a variety of tracking strategies intermittently to keep student interest.

Learning Styles

Models: Students build models of what they are learning. They label and explain their models.

PMP (Perceptual Modality Preferences) to Students: The teacher teaches students that people have visual, auditory, and/or tactile/kinesthetic perceptual preferences. They learn to monitor their own preferences and take some responsibility for creating the best learning experience for themselves. They also learn to style flex to match the style a teacher is using at a given point in time. The teacher pledges to provide learning opportunities for the students who learn best by seeing things, those who prefer touching or experiencing something, and those who learn best by hearing things.

Style Flex: The teacher explains that he wants to address the learning style of all of the students in the class but acknowledges that it is impossible to do so in a given moment. Thus, the teacher states that he or she will work to meet all styles over time but that the students need to *style flex* when the teacher is not teaching to their given style. Style flex means the student will shift to match the style of learning to the style the teacher is teaching at the time.

Tactile Sort: Information from the curriculum is printed in a large font, one copy per student or group of students. Then the teacher cuts or tears them apart. Students put them back together. Students can also make their own puzzles and they can exchange them with other students.

Thinking Skills

Acrostic: Students use letters of a concept to summarize the content learned. Legislature becomes: *L*aws, *E*lected officials, *G*rouped into two branches, and so on. This promotes thinking at the synthesis level of Bloom's Taxonomy.

Advance Organizer: This is an outline with the details missing. In the form of statements or questions it helps the learner organize the learning by knowing the key concepts or questions in advance. This promotes thinking at the analysis level of Bloom's Taxonomy.

Balloon Bat: Everyone is given a balloon and a small (1 inch by 8½ inches) piece of paper. Each student is asked to think back over what he has learned and choose one item he thinks most important. He writes this item on the paper, rolls the paper up, and inserts it into the balloon. Next each person blows up his balloon and ties it closed. Everyone forms a circle, notes the color of their balloon and then listens for the signal from the teacher to begin. When they hear, "Ready, bat!" they bat the balloons to one another. When the stop signal is given, everyone grabs a balloon, taking care to not get his own color. Students form the circle again. On a signal everyone breaks his balloon. The student to the left of the teacher reads the strip that was in his balloon. This is repeated until all ideas have been stated. (Note: It is thoughtful to give students permission to cover their ears and step back a little if loud noises cause them discomfort. Popping balloons can be very noisy. It is also very important to pick up all of the debris from the broken balloons.) This promotes thinking at the knowledge level of Bloom's Taxonomy.

Blitz a List: The teacher creates sequential lists of key learning over a period of time, placing them in the classroom where all students can see them. He uses the list as an aid to review and spiraling of key concepts. This promotes thinking at the knowledge level of Bloom's Taxonomy.

Bloom's Taxonomy to Students: Students learn the categories of Bloom's Taxonomy and use it as a framework for organizing the thinking skill strategies they learn. This promotes thinking at all levels of Bloom's Taxonomy. It also helps the students gain skills in metacognition.

Brainstorm: Students generate and share as many ideas on a specific topic as they can in a designated period of time. All ideas are accepted initially. Then the teacher gives some criteria for the best kind of ideas for the assignment and the students process the ideas to determine which ones they can use to accomplish their assigned task. This promotes thinking at the synthesis and evaluation level of Bloom's Taxonomy.

Glows and Grows: Students examine a list of skills or information relative to a unit they have just studied. Then they categorize this list into *glows* and *grows.* Glows are those skills or information the student assesses he has mastered. Grows are those skills or content learning in which the student thinks he still needs to "grow or improve." This promotes thinking skills at the evaluation level of Bloom's Taxonomy.

CLOD: The teacher checks for the Correct Level of Difficulty for a particular student or a full class by asking questions such as "What do we know about . . . ?" or by giving an introductory quiz that finds out what students know. This promotes thinking at the comprehension level of Bloom's Taxonomy.

Concentration: Students work in small groups to compose a set of 10 question-and-answer cards—one color for questions and one color for answers. They exchange cards with another small group and play concentration by laying the cards out on the table face down and taking turns at matching a question with the correct answer. When a match is made the cards are moved to the side of the table. The game is not competitive. Instead each person is trying to concentrate to see where the matches are so that when his turn comes he can get a match for the team. The goal is to match all questions and answers. This promotes thinking at the comprehension level of Bloom's Taxonomy.

Exit Visa: Before leaving the classroom, students must identify one thing they have learned during a designated period of time (that day, that week, etc.). This can be by writing or orally. They also indicate how they will use this information. It can be fun and challenging to do it orally, and to set the criteria that nothing can be said twice. To prevent panic or damage of self-esteem for those at the end of the sharing, it is advisable to let the last 10 students use their notes or books. This promotes thinking at the application level of Bloom's Taxonomy.

KWL: The teacher provides a three-column Advanced Organizer where students record what they *K*now, what they *W*ant to know when they have finished, and what they have *L*earned about a topic they are studying. This promotes thinking at the analysis level of Bloom's Taxonomy.

Payoffs/Problems: As the learning process begins, the students are asked to fold a piece of paper in half and to label one half *Payoffs* and the other half *Problems*. They are then asked to predict what they think they will gain from what they are about to learn, and they record these on the half of the page labeled *Payoffs*. Next they predict what they think their problems will be and these are recorded on the second half of the page. If time permits the teacher may want to work with the students individually to plan how to overcome these potential problems. The page is saved so at the end of the learning experience the students can use it to record what they actually gained, what were the problems, and how did those problems impact the learning positively or negatively. An extension of this idea is to ask the students how they will deal with such problems when they meet them in the future. This promotes thinking at the evaluation level of Bloom's Taxonomy.

PMI (Positive, Minus, Interesting):   At the end of an activity or learning experience the learners identify what was plus (or positive) about the learning, what was minus (or negative), and what was interesting. The responses are recorded. This promotes thinking at the evaluation level of Bloom's Taxonomy.

Rapid Row Relay: Students sit in rows and the teacher gives the first person in each row a topic or a question on a piece of paper. The students either brainstorm information about the topic or answer the question. The first person records his ideas and hands the paper to the student sitting behind him. This process continues until one row wins by being the first to have all students in that row respond. The teacher reviews the final product to insure quality and accuracy. The students in the winning row receive a prize or a privilege. This is thinking at the knowledge level of Bloom's Taxonomy.

Read, Pair, Share: Students read a given assignment individually. They then pair with a partner and share answers. A combined answer can then be shared with the entire group. This strategy can be used with a small amount of reading material or a large amount. If it is a large amount of material the teacher should pace the reading and sharing intervals.

RTW (Read, Think, Write):   Students read designated information, think about that information, and then record their understanding of that information. This promotes thinking at the knowledge and comprehension levels.

Review Whip: Start in any spot in the room and identify a pattern of progression. Each student states something he has learned in a designated period of time. An advanced form of this is to have each student write three or four questions. The teacher asks the first question and designates a student to answer it. The student answers and then asks one of his own questions of the student to his left. This process continues until all students have asked and answered a question. The questions can be collected and used on a test. If students know Bloom's Taxonomy, the questions can be designated as higher-level questions. This promotes thinking at all levels of Bloom's Taxonomy.

Sculpt a Concept (Living Sculpture):   Students form a nonverbal representation of the concepts they are studying. This can be a moving sculpture or a stationary one. This is thinking at the synthesis level of Bloom's Taxonomy.

Snowball Fight: Students write a question to which they have learned the answer on a sheet of paper. They repeat the process on a second piece of paper with a different question. The class is divided into two groups and they face each other at opposite sides of the room. They crumple their two pages and, at the signal, throw the "snowball" at the other team. They can scoop snowballs off the floor and continue to throw at the other team. When the teacher calls the stop signal, all throwing stops. The snowballs are counted and a winner declared. One student is designated to uncrumple his snowball and read the question. He answers the question and then the student who authored the just-answered question goes next. This process continues until all students have answered a question. This promotes thinking at the recall and comprehension levels of Bloom's Taxonomy.

Songs as Summary: Students use a familiar tune to create their own lyrics summarizing what they have learned about a topic. They can do this individually or in small groups. This promotes thinking at the comprehension and synthesis levels of Bloom's Taxonomy.

T-Chart: Teachers provide or students create a T-chart with the label of a concept or skill on the top and one side of the T labeled *Looks Like* and the other labeled *Sounds Like*. Students fill in both sides and then write a definition of the concept. This promotes thinking at the comprehension level of Bloom's Taxonomy.

Think/Ink/Speak: Students are asked a question and they mentally process the answer. Then they write the answer, and finally the teacher designates one student to verbally give the answer. During the writing step the teacher can easily monitor and check for understanding with several students. This promotes thinking at the comprehension level of Bloom's Taxonomy.

Venn Diagram: Draw two overlapping circles. One concept is written in one circle; a different concept is written in the second circle. Descriptors specific to each concept are written in their respective circles. Descriptors shared by both concepts are written in the overlapping area. This promotes thinking at the analysis level of Bloom's Taxonomy.

Wall Grid: Concepts or content material can be placed on an x and y axis to demonstrate the connection between and among the concepts and content material. This promotes thinking at the analysis and evaluation levels of Bloom's Taxonomy.

About the Authors

Frederic Skoglund is the founder and president of Viking Solutions, a consulting group serving the educational community. His primary work is focused on assisting school leaders to improve teacher performance and elevate student achievement. He also works at the district level developing teacher evaluation instruments and intervention programs. He lives in Mesa, Arizona. He can be reached at fskoglund@aol.com. Visit his website at www.vikingsolutions.com

Judy Ness is the president of Judy Ness, Inc., a consulting service focused on district and school improvement. Her training provides facilitators with content and tools to work with district and school leaders to improve student achievement. She has also coauthored *Putting Sense into Consensus* and *Tips and Tools for Trainers and Teams*. She lives in Seattle, Washington. She can be reached at ness@cablespeed.com.

CPSIA information can be obtained at www.ICGtesting.com
261785BV00005B/3/P